How to
Teach
Reading

When You're Not
a Reading Teacher

By Sharon H. Faber

Incentive Publications, Inc.
Nashville, Tennessee

*"If I'd a knowed what a trouble it is
to make a book I wouldn't a tackled it
and ain't a goin' to no more."*

— Mark Twain

Acknowledgment

For all their unconditional love and support, I want to thank:

*my mother, Nelda Strong, who has always been
my role model, inspiration, and the best mom a girl could have;*

my children, Robert and Julie, who are the pride and joy of my life;

*and my husband, Conrad,
who is my soul mate, best friend, and the love of my life.*

*Illustrated by Marta J. Drayton
Cover by Rebecca Rüegger
Edited by Jennifer J. Streams and Charlotte Bosarge*

Library of Congress Control Number: 2003113122
ISBN 0-86530-605-2

1   2   3   4   5   6   7   8   9   10   07   06   05   04

PRINTED IN THE UNITED STATES OF AMERICA
www.incentivepublications.com

Table of Contents

INTRODUCTION

"There are no areas of the brain that specialize in reading. Reading is probably the most difficult task we ask the brain to undertake."

— David Sousa

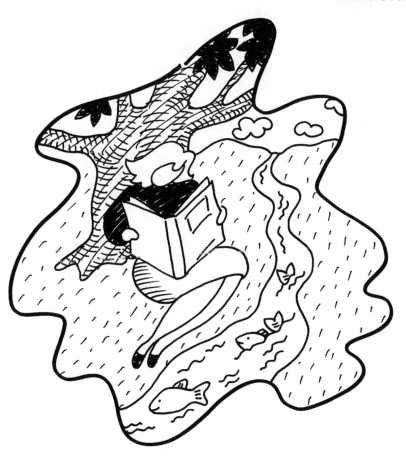

I was not trained as a reading teacher. I was an English major who became an English teacher. Being a teacher was something I wanted to do since I was a little girl with four younger brothers who let me "pretend" that I was their teacher. After graduating from college, my plan was simple: I wanted to teach the subject I loved and instill that same love into the hearts and minds of all my students. I dreamed of making the classic books, plays, and poetry come alive for them as they always had for me. I was going to share my passion and inspire them to love and appreciate literature as part of their lives.

When I finally became a middle school teacher, I got the biggest shock of my life. Not only were many of my students unenthused about both school and my English class, but some of them couldn't even read! It had never occurred to me that I would get students who would be struggling readers or even non-readers. I thought that all children learned to read in kindergarten and first grade— at least by they time they were out of elementary school! How could I be getting kids this age who couldn't even read? I was trained to be an English teacher; I wasn't trained to be a reading teacher.

Even worse, I found that some students could read and pronounce the words in their assignments, but when we discussed the content of what they had read, it was as if they had never done the reading. It was painfully clear to me that some of my so-called "best" readers were only "word-callers"! They could recognize the words, but they struggled (or failed) to extract meaning from what they had read. Some of these students even made good grades. I was amazed that they been so successful in school without being able to truly comprehend what they had read.

I had so many questions:

- How did these students get so far in school in the first place?
- How could I teach students to appreciate literary content when they couldn't even read a short story or a simple poem—let alone a whole book?
- What was I supposed to do with these students?

For many teachers, teaching strategies are intuitive and based simply on the need to cope with day-to-day challenges in the classroom, i.e., the "strategy" evolves as the day evolves. Therefore, if a student cannot read, the teacher "covers" by making the textbook or content come alive for the entire class, making the non-readers' lack of reading skill irrelevant. Teachers will make sure that students learn the important, basic content, but are rarely able (or trained) to address the fundamental issue at hand: If they cannot read, they cannot comprehend content.

For years, many teachers have used reading strategies without realizing what they were doing. Every time a teacher breaks down a textbook into manageable units, highlights the features of a textbook, or provides specific content-related vocabulary from a textbook, that teacher is using a reading strategy.

Of course teachers recognize that most students who cannot read are instead smart in many other ways: They can recite every word verbatim from their favorite movies or CDs, or are quite surprisingly skilled at imitating their teachers' facial expressions, voices, and mannerisms. Since their lack of reading skills are sometimes the only deterrent to class instruction, teachers assign projects, group work, graphic organizers, tapes, videos, or anything they can think of to help the students learn using different modalities. Additionally, teachers are so pressured and preoccupied with reaching state standards, state tests, and achievement scores that they often forget that students who do not score well may be under-performing because they cannot *read* the actual questions on the test—not because they were not taught the material.

In this way, many well-meaning teachers unknowingly set their struggling readers up for future failure by doing two things:

- Not dealing with the problems for students in their own classroom

- Allowing students with reading disabilities to move forward to the next teacher (who may not care if they cannot read)

Good teachers—in all content areas—must adopt the attitude that any child who comes into their class with a reading disability is one thing: their responsibility. Teachers must show students how to use thinking and reading strategies that will enable them to comprehend the content as well as the individual words. Teachers must model thinking processes when reading for content so students can learn by example. Teachers must show students how great writers, historians, scientists, and mathematicians process information and arrive at conclusions.

If you are worried that this practice will inhibit individual student creativity, here is an example: In school, student teachers are forced to create extensive lesson plans to show if and how they can apply what they have learned. This type of assignment forces student teachers to think carefully about every step in the teaching process and choose the specific strategies that will work best for each different type of content or lesson. In teaching reading to middle school students, as well as teaching student teachers, creativity comes only after mastering the fundamentals. Learning to read is a process, and content is the vehicle teachers use to drive that process toward creativity and comprehension.

For any teacher who has a student who cannot read, for every teacher who has never been taught how to teach reading, and for every teacher who loves their students and wants each of them to be successful in life, this book will be useful. Outlines provided in the book are strategies that, when used on a regular basis, will help all students become better at reading. However, for students to become good readers, they must first read, write, speak, and listen to something, and that something is the content of the subject areas.

In *How to Teach Reading When You're Not a Reading Teacher,* my goal is to make middle grades teachers aware of which reading strategies they already use, then introduce and amplify additional strategies they can incorporate into any subject area. Using current research on teaching reading and how students learn, the practical approach presented here is focused primarily on teaching reading to 10- to 14-year-olds. Also included are notes about the important physical, intellectual, emotional, and social development of middle grades children— something every middle grades teachers should understand in order to meet their students' needs as learners. So, before we talk about reading, let's talk about the kids.

 **DID YOU KNOW?** Researcher David Bloom says that 13 is the most critical age for students because of hormones, peer pressures, and social forces.

As Teddy Roosevelt once said, "Whenever you are asked if you can do a job, tell 'em, 'Certainly I can!' Then get busy and find out how to do it." That is what this book is all about. We are going to get busy and find out how to teach reading when you're not a reading teacher!

What Kind of Readers Are at the Middle Level?

> *"Do what you can, with what you have,*
> *where you are."*
> — Teddy Roosevelt

After I had been teaching a few years, I began to be able to identify my students' reading ability as early as the first day of school, and I could do this without their ever having to open a book! Based on my experience, I developed a theory that I think may be true on the first day of school for all middle grades teachers. I call it "The Three Reading Groups Theory." My "scientific method" was to hypothesize that my students generally fell into one of three groups, and I defined these groups by where the students chose to sit on the first day of school, before I made my seating chart. Think about your classes and see if this description fits your students.

Kids Who Choose Desks in the Front of the Room

The kids who choose to sit in the front of the room come from homes that are more like their teachers' homes. They probably have parents who value education and school success. These are the kids who have been read to, and who have homes with magazines, books, and newspapers available to them. Their parents have taught them the rules of school, such as: be attentive, do your homework, do not make crude noises in public, be polite and respectful to the teacher, and raise your hand before you answer a question. These kids come to school and know that learning is important. In fact, these are the kids who make a teacher's job so enjoyable. They always say things like, "I love school; I love to learn; You are my favorite teacher." What teachers do not realize (or maybe we do) is that these students go to every one of their teachers and tell them the same things. In teacher terms, these students are "reading ready."

Kids Who Choose Desks in the Middle of the Room

The students who choose to sit in the middle of the room are almost as delightful as the students up front. The only real difference I have found with the kids in the middle is that they choose to do *only* as much work or to behave *only* as well as will keep teachers off their cases. They tend to be realists who know they have to go to school because that's what kids do; it's the law. They come to school every day to see their friends, they do the required work at a minimal level, and they behave right to the limits of their teachers' tolerance levels. Most students are in this middle group, and in teacher terms, they are "almost reading ready."

Kids Who Choose Desks in the Back of the Room

As most educators know, the farther back in class students sit, the more at-risk the students become. The kids who choose these seats want to be invisible—they want to disappear into the back wall and they do not want teachers to mess with them. Many of them have attitude problems. Their body language often says it all; they have their heads on their desks or they are slouched over their desks with their legs stretched out and their faces reflecting a bored expression. By the time they get to middle school, for many of these students, it isn't "I cannot read," it has become, "I *will not* read."

These kids have to save face at all costs. No wonder some of them have become discipline problems. School has not been a good place for them to be, and for any number of reasons (many out of the teacher's control), they have decided they will simply stay in school until they are old enough to drop out. In teacher terms, they are "not reading ready, highly at risk of failure, and probably struggling or non-readers." Our prisons are full of people who dropped out of school, and, sadly, some of these kids have the potential to become one of those statistics.

Year after year, I saw these same three reading groups in my classes, and I did everything I could to make the class a successful experience for all of them. Until the last few years, I thought I had done a good job, but when I began to learn about teaching reading, I found I could have done so much more.

After recognizing that students fit into the three reading groups, it suddenly occurred to me that there were struggling readers in all three groups, at different times. The students' ability to read actually depended on the text they were reading. Even good readers struggled when they read difficult or unknown text. (I still remember how I hated my statistics book in college and how hard I struggled to make sense out of all that gibberish!) I found many of my students—although they could already read at varying levels—also needed to be taught specifically what they were doing as they read successfully, so they could help themselves later when text became more difficult.

This book is a compilation of the ideas and strategies collected from many sources over many years, organized in a way that busy teachers will find useful. Since there is no one "best way" to teach reading (or anything else for that matter), tailor these techniques to your curriculum, your students, and your teaching style. In other words, take what you want and leave the rest.

There are many explanations for why some kids cannot read by the time they are in middle school. However, one of the reasons is often that when they were taught to read in elementary school, they were not ready to learn the skills. Just like their teachers, students are all very different. They come to us in all shapes and sizes and, especially in the case of middle graders, at a difficult time in their lives. It is our job to take them where they are developmentally (physically, intellectually, emotionally, and socially) and help them become the best learners they can be. *It is important to teach reading strategies intentionally.* If teachers truly believe that they make a difference—and I do—then teaching our students reading skills and strategies must become an important part of teaching them in every subject. This book is my way of sharing ideas that I have collected on how middle school teachers can accomplish this awesome task.

"Setting a goal is not the main thing. It is deciding how you will go about achieving it and staying with that plan."

— Tom Landry, football coach

THE
RESEARCH

"To begin with the end in mind means to start with a clear understanding of your destination. It means to know where you're going so that you better understand where you are now so that the steps you take are always in the right direction."

— Stephen Covey

What Is Your Reading I.Q.?

Based on prior knowledge about reading comprehension, complete this pre-assessment about reading theories and strategies. Answer each question even if you are not certain of the answer. By the time you finish this book, you will know the correct answers. Some of them may even surprise you.

Reading Quiz

T or F   1. Content reading strategies are useful only with printed text.

T or F   2. When good readers read, they look at every letter and every word.

T or F   3. If students have not developed a strong inner voice, they will mumble out loud and move their lips when they read.

T or F   4. Eye focus is an important element of learning to read.

T or F   5. Students have difficulty reading aloud and comprehending at the same time.

T or F   6. Prior knowledge is an important part of reading comprehension.

T or F   7. Reading comprehension is "experience with the text and a search for meaning."

T or F   8. Comprehension is selective. Good readers focus on important information and poor readers focus only on their interest in the text being read.

T or F   9. Good readers examine the structure of words and use roots and affixes to help comprehend new words.

T or F 10. When teaching a reading strategy, the content used must be easily comprehended and not overly interesting.

What Research Tells Us

"That the brain learns to read at all attests to its remarkable ability to sift through seemingly confusing input and establish patterns and systems. For a few children, this process comes naturally; most have to be taught."

— David Sousa

Learning to read text is both a difficult and unnatural process for the brain. According to the National Institute for Literacy and the Center for Education Statistics, over 40 million adults in the United States are functionally illiterate, and approximately 40% of 4th graders lack the most basic reading skills. Walberg and Tsai identified a phenomenon in education that is called the "Matthew Effect" (Walberg and Tsai, 1983) which is based on the line from the Bible that says that "the rich get richer and the poor get poorer." It means that the gap between children who are good readers and those who are poor readers gets wider and wider as they move through school. Those who cannot read fall farther and farther behind their peers and are then less and less motivated to become good readers. In fact, high school graduation rates can be predicted with reasonable accuracy by assessing a child's reading skill at the end of 3rd grade. If a child is not reading on grade level by the 4th grade, he is quite unlikely to graduate from high school.

 **DID YOU KNOW?** If students are identified as low-achieving by the 3rd grade, they remain in that group throughout their schooling unless a future teacher recognizes their potential.

CHAPTER 1

The National Reading Panel (2000) defined reading comprehension as "intentional thinking during which meaning is constructed through interaction between the text and the reader." The panel also explained that "the content of meaning is influenced by the text and by the reader's prior knowledge and experience that are brought to bear on it" and that "reading is purposeful and active." In other words, readers derive meaning from text when they engage in intentional, problem-solving thinking processes. Reading comprehension can be improved by instruction in using specific cognitive strategies or in using reasoning strategies when encountering barriers to understanding.

Comprehension has two levels, literal comprehension and higher-order comprehension. Literal comprehension is identifying individual words and their meanings, as determined by immediate context. Higher-order comprehension is when analytic, evaluative, and reflective comprehension occurs. The skills necessary to achieve literal comprehension are just as important as those necessary for the higher-order comprehension processes. For children to become good readers, they must develop a number of skills that work together during the reading process. Children should be taught reading in developmentally appropriate ways in their zone of proximal development. To ensure that all children can read, there must be focused instruction from knowledgeable and skilled teachers at all grade levels.

The National Reading Panel also issued a report in 2000, "Teaching Children to Read," which identified key skills and methods important to reading achievement. The members of the panel reviewed more than 100,000 studies that related to reading success. The report provided analysis and discussion in five areas of reading instruction: phonemic awareness, phonics, vocabulary development, fluency, and text comprehension. Each skill was defined, the evidence from the research was reviewed, and implications for classroom instruction were given along with descriptions of proven strategies for teaching each skill. In order for kids to learn to read well, explicit and systematic instruction must be provided in all five areas.

Area 1: Phonemic Awareness

For most content area teachers (as opposed to a trained reading teacher or an elementary teacher), phonemic awareness is a new concept. What is phonemic awareness? All these big words mean is that in order to be able to read, kids must be able to hear the sounds that letters make when they are put together to make words. When letter sounds are written in books, they look like this: /b/. The marks on each side mean that you say the sound but not the letter name, so the word "bat" would be written /b/a/t/ if you wanted to show that you should say the word phonemically, i.e., using the letter sounds. This is the kind of thing that kindergarten and first grade teachers do with students all the time when they teach them the letters in the alphabet and how to put the letters together with their sounds to make words. The sounds of the letters are called phonemes.

Students need to know that all spoken words consist of these phonemes, or individual sounds. They need to see how words can be segmented (pulled apart) into sounds, and how these sounds can be blended (put back together) and manipulated (added, deleted, and substituted) to create and read a variety of words. Students need to know how to use phonemic awareness to blend sounds to read words and to segment sounds in words to spell them. In order to use phonemic awareness, students must know letter-sound correspondences, spelling patterns, syllables, and meaningful word parts. Phonemic awareness is important because it improves children's word reading and reading comprehension while simultaneously helping children learn to spell.

Area 2: Phonics

The second important element for reading is phonics. Many teachers today had phonics in their reading instruction classes when they were in college. Phonics is the relationship between the sounds heard when spoken (phonemes) and the letters in the alphabet (graphemes). If children are to benefit from phonics instruction, they first need phonemic awareness. Children who cannot hear and work with the phonemes of spoken words will have a difficult time learning how to relate these phonemes to the graphemes when they see them in written form. Children who are able to understand how sounds and letters work together to make words can usually recognize familiar words and are often better able to decode unfamiliar words.

Phonics instruction teaches children a system for remembering how to read words. The alphabetic system is a mnemonic device that helps children learn to identify words. It increases their ability to comprehend what they read because reading words automatically and accurately enables students to focus on the meaning of the text instead of the decoding of the words. The effects of phonics instruction on older students are limited to improving their word reading and oral text reading skills. The effects do not extend to spelling and reading comprehension.

While most teachers have heard the term "phonics" and have a general idea of what phonics are, at the middle school level teachers usually do not teach phonics to students except to occasionally help them sound out a new word. It is likely that any teacher who helps students sound out words does it because he was taught that way when they were in school—not because he knows how to teach phonics. If that is true, it is also likely that teachers who were not taught to sound out words when they learned to read, probably do not know how to teach their students to do it.

Area 3: Vocabulary Development

Vocabulary development involves teaching kids to store information about the meanings and pronunciation of words necessary to understand a given content. Many teachers think that vocabulary development means giving students words only in the content area that they need to know, having them look up the definitions in the dictionary, writing their own sentences using the words, and/or having them find the words in sentences in the textbook or whatever text they are reading. Some teachers even go so far as to teach students the difference in the denotation (dictionary definition) and connotation (real-life usage) of the words. Once the process of teaching reading becomes clear, it is obvious that just having students do these things does not really mean that they will *learn* the words. The result is a group of students who can pass a weekly test but will not recognize many of the words or retain what the words meant two weeks later.

Area 4: Fluency (Including Oral Reading Skills)

Fluency is coordinating word recognition speed and accuracy and the comprehension of connected text (Burns, Griffin, and Snow, 1999). Fluency means that students can read text accurately and quickly, while simultaneously making a connection between the words and comprehension of what the words mean. Fluency also means that when students are reading aloud they can group words into meaningful phrases, observe punctuation, read with expression, and read the words with the proper inflection so that a listener can enjoy the reading. Their reading sounds natural, as if they were speaking. Fluency changes depending on what material readers are reading and their familiarity with the words and text. Even skilled readers may not be able to read some texts, like legal or technical material, fluently.

Fluency is important because it provides a bridge between recognizing words and comprehension. Fluent readers do not have to concentrate on decoding words so they can focus their attention on the content. They make connections between the ideas in the text and their own personal experience and knowledge as they read. Less fluent readers must focus longer on figuring out the words, leaving little time, attention, or energy to comprehend the text.

At the middle grades level, there are many students who can say the words when they read them, but their reading aloud is a painful experience for those listening because they lack fluency. They read slowly, word by word, and their oral reading is choppy and plodding.

Area 5: Reading Comprehension Strategies

Reading comprehension strategies are sets of steps that good readers use to make sense of what they are reading. These strategies help good readers understand, remember, and explain to others what they have read. The only problem with comprehension strategies is that good readers tend to use them without really thinking about what they are doing. These strategies can be taught to students, but teachers must know the steps to teach them. Classroom teachers must learn what the effective reading strategies are, what steps are involved in each strategy, and how to model the steps themselves so that students can mimic them when they read.

Reading strategies need to be flexible and adaptable to meet the needs of any reading problem regardless of the content. Many factors like topic familiarity (prior knowledge), text and picture support, number of unfamiliar words, and teacher support are also important in reading comprehension. Remember that good readers use a variety of strategies when they read. It is the teacher's responsibility to help students learn which strategies work particularly well for each type of content.

Translating the Research Into Practice

Our brains remember what is used frequently, and students develop procedural knowledge through repeated practice or rehearsals. As students practice recalling facts or procedures, the material becomes part of their long-term memory and, therefore, automatic. While some "drill" is important, students who employ strategies to recall information tend to remember what they have learned. Teachers must provide a wide range of activities and offer various strategy options for students. These options will allow them to become familiar with forms and uses of written language, to develop language and meta-cognition skills required for comprehension, to learn how words are structured and represented in print, and to become enthusiastic about learning to read and write. Then, they will be equipped with skills that they can use in new situations or when the learning becomes more difficult.

At the middle grades level, content area teachers find many students who have trouble expressing themselves effectively in reading and writing. Many students cannot think critically about what they read, and therefore are unable to either make inferences from their reading or process complex material. For these students, teachers must begin with basic reading strategies. Then, all students must practice the basic reading strategies, repeating them until they become automatic. A primary goal for all teachers should be to make sure that students use the appropriate reading strategies for each type of content.

For students to become good readers, they need to learn comprehension strategies that will teach them:

- How to read narrative and expository text

- How to understand and retain what they read

- How to connect their own knowledge and experience to the text

- How to use comprehension strategies flexibly and in combination

- How to do whatever it takes to understand, organize, and remember what is read

- How to communicate with others about what is read

A great deal of research has been done in the areas of teaching, learning, and reading over the past 30 years. During the past 10 years, research by neuroscientists has expanded what we know about those areas in relation to the human brain. Scientists have studied which brain areas are most active during which types of educational tasks (Sousa, 1999). Specialists have identified brain regions that are associated with learning activities such as language, reading, math, motor learning, music appreciation, or verbal responses to questions in a classroom discussion (Sousa, 2001). This extensive research has provided educators with some consistent answers to what types of instructional strategies work best and what should be done in schools and classrooms to improve student achievement.

One common theme in the research is that the best practice in instructional strategies depends on what the learner will do with what they are learning. Therefore, it is clear that students need to learn in ways that will allow them to retain what they have learned.

In their book, *Classroom Instruction That Works: Research-Based Strategies for Increasing Student Achievement*, Marzano, Pickering, and Pollack (ASCD, 2001), identified nine categories of instructional strategies that were proven to improve student achievement:

1. Identifying similarities and differences

2. Summarizing and note taking

3. Reinforcing effort and providing recognition

4. Completing homework

5. Representing knowledge

6. Participating in learning groups

7. Setting objectives and providing feedback

8. Generating and testing hypotheses

9. Using cues, questions, and advance organizers

Variations of these nine instructional strategies are found throughout the research on reading, and a number of these instructional practices are rooted in brain-compatible research (Sousa, 1999). However, it is important to note that while these instructional strategies are useful for teachers, students must *both* be involved with their own learning and take personal responsibility for their achievement.

"Patience is a necessary ingredient of genius."

— Benjamin Disraeli

CONTENT AREA
READING

*"You can read to a child and he is
 entertained for a while,
But if you teach a child to read,
he can learn for a lifetime."*

— Conrad Faber

What Is Content Area Reading?

Content area reading means helping students make connections between what they already know and the new information being presented. This helps students create meaning and comprehend what they are reading. Content teachers need to teach their students how to use reading as a tool for thinking and learning in their specific subject. They must help students read their textbooks and additional materials effectively in order to understand and learn the content. Teachers must do much more than just assign pages to read, lecture, or ask questions to see if students have read the assignment. They must help students link reading and learning across the content areas.

To get good at something, one must do that thing often and practice. Thus, to become a good reader, a student must read. Reading is an interaction that happens among the reader, the text, and the content. When they read a great deal, students become good readers. Unfortunately, at the middle grades level, many middle grades students only read when their teachers make them read. Without practice, students have trouble reading in content area classes for a variety of reasons. They often have trouble understanding the author's ideas, and since they have not had much experience with the topic, they cannot make connections with their personal lives and, therefore, create meaning from new ideas. In addition, struggling readers think the reading materials are too hard or too boring to begin with because they do not have effective reading skills to figure it out.

When students come into class with these kinds of reading problems, content area teachers need to answer the following questions:

1. What are the specific skills or knowledge that students need to read the content material effectively?

2. What environment promotes effective reading and learning?

3. What strategies can I use with my students to help them in my subject area?

Three Factors That Affect Student Learning

At the middle grades level, teachers deal with content area literacy. This is the level of reading and writing necessary for students to read and comprehend the instructional materials used in the content areas. Content area literacy engages students in learning new knowledge. Up until now, most students have been learning to read, and now they must use their reading skills to learn the content of their subjects—they must read to learn. In simple terms, there are three main factors for content area teachers to consider. The three things that affect content area learning are the teacher, the student, and the content.

Factor One: The Teacher

As in all learning, the most important factor is the teacher. In the middle grades classroom, the teacher must have a sound understanding of the subject matter, how students learn, pedagogy, and how to motivate students to learn. Another thing the teacher must add to this knowledge base, in order to help students read content material, is an understanding of the reading process itself. Finally, middle grades teachers must understand the specific developmental characteristics of the students they teach. When it is understood that most of the things that middle grades students do to drive teachers crazy are perfectly normal behaviors for this age group, teachers can better understand how to teach them.

Teachers must take an active role in both the teaching and the learning process. They must motivate, instruct, and guide their students as they try to learn in their classes. They must help students learn to monitor what makes sense as they read, how the new information connects with what they already know, and how they learn best. Middle grades teachers must provide strategies to help students organize and systematize new learning. By doing so, the students can become active learners who gain accurate, lasting, and useful knowledge.

Teaching reading is complex. It requires a good knowledge of research and how to apply it, and it takes time and hard work to practice it effectively. And to teach effectively, middle grades teachers must connect what needs to be learned with the students' lives and interests, i.e., connect the new to the familiar. This means teachers must know their students and the cultures in which they live. All students come to the classroom with different backgrounds, and they construct their own understanding of what they are learning based on their prior social and academic experiences. They bring with them what they have learned outside the classroom and what they have already learned in school. It is the role of the teacher to help students understand their own thinking as they are required to explain, clarify, or make predictions about what they are learning. Planning balanced instruction for diversity requires that teachers are knowledgeable about the research and make informed decisions about their students' needs and about reading instruction.

The goal is to get students to think *as they read*. This requires that teachers get students actively engaged in the learning process. The best way to do this is to get them interested and excited about what they are learning. This interest and excitement will happen if teachers are passionate and enthusiastic about what they teach and, then, pass that enthusiasm on to their students.

Factor Two: The Student

The second factor that impacts learning is the student and what each one brings with him to the classroom. The student's prior knowledge and experiences, language development, reading ability, and attitudes toward school are all critical elements in content area learning. As any middle grades teacher knows, working with these students is a challenge for many reasons: middle grades kids have unique physical, intellectual, emotional, and social characteristics and issues. Knowing the characteristics of this age group is imperative for middle grades teachers. While it is tempting for middle grades teachers to say they know their students "because they work with them day after day"—how many of them have actually studied the characteristics of transescents in today's society? Those who have not need to do so.

Students who just memorize information generally do not retain that information in long-term memory. (Those of us who memorized for tests, made our A's, but now remember nothing, know how true this is!) If middle grades students are expected to perform something automatically (e.g., multiplication tables, spelling rules, or formulas), repetition, drill, and practice will work. However, for more complex and extended content to be stored in long-term memory, it is vital for students to understand what they are learning. This means that a teacher must include those teaching strategies that advance student understanding of concepts. This way, not only can students remember what they have learned, but also they will be able to apply what they have learned in new situations, such as taking standardized tests.

Content area teachers need to know which reading skills are best for *their* students to understand *their* material. They need to help students by teaching study skills and effective strategies for reading, writing, organizing, and test taking. Readers construct meaning as they read. Good readers predict, organize information, and interact with the text. They evaluate what they are reading based on what they already know. They change how they read based on what they are reading and if they are having any problems understanding the reading. Teachers must provide support for all students to succeed as readers in their content areas, or both the teacher and the students will become frustrated and feel like they have failed. The bottom line to teaching content area reading is first knowing to whom you are teaching it.

Factor Three: The Content

The third factor essential for learning to occur is the content—the text and materials used in classes. The text's quality, clarity, writing style, scope and sequence, content, format, organization, and patterns are critical (Barton and Billmeyer, 1998). The materials used as the vehicles for the content are very important and need to be selected and taught with care. One of the reasons this is important is that many middle grades students perform well on teachers' tests during the year, but when they take the standardized tests, their scores do not reflect what teachers thought the students had learned. There seems to be very little transfer of learning to new situations if the content itself is not complete, interesting, and meaningful.

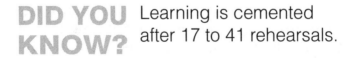

DID YOU KNOW? Learning is cemented after 17 to 41 rehearsals.

How Is Content Area Reading Taught?

When thinking about content area reading with the middle grades teacher, the middle grades student, and middle grades content in mind, it becomes very clear that teachers in every subject must help students by supporting them before, during, and after their reading experience. "Once students reach the intermediate grades, they meet approximately 10,000 new words—words never before encountered in print—in school reading each year. Most of these words are big words, words of seven or more letters and two or more syllables" (Cunningham, 1999).

Every teacher needs to start reading content from a middle grades student's perspective—not from her own personal perspective of studying and possibly teaching that subject for years. Every teacher needs to take a routine, fresh look at what is taught, and every teacher should assume that "if I have not taught it, my students do not know it." Pretend that the material is written in a foreign language (for many students this is what textbooks look like). The challenge is to figure out how to understand the reading anyway. This may sound bizarre, but looking at the content through the students' eyes helps teachers to better determine which strategies students will need if they are to construct meaning from what they are reading in class. Content area reading is the most effective of all these techniques.

Three Important Elements for Content Area Reading

The brain has three methods it uses to remember things: mnemonic, structural, and semantic. In mnemonic tasks, students are taught to group words by sound. In structural tasks, students are taught to group words by the alphabet, and in semantic tasks, students learn to group things by meaning. Rates of memory are better when words are grouped into categories by meaning, or semantically. In other words, students can improve memory by giving meaning to what they are expected to know—they understand it.

Just like learning, reading is an active process because comprehension requires more than reading the words on a page. Effective readers interact with the text *while* they read it. They work to make sense of what they are reading, and they apply strategies to understand the information when the reading gets too difficult for them.

When students read, there are three things a content area teacher must use to plan lessons:

1. Prior Knowledge

2. The Classroom Learning Environment

3. Text Features

1. Prior Knowledge

Prior knowledge is the content knowledge and personal experience that a reader brings to the text. As stated before, when students read new information, they make sense of it by seeing how it connects with what they already know. Students do not bring the same backgrounds or experiences to school, so no two of them will comprehend anything they read the same way. Reading for meaning is not the same as what many students do—simply move their eyes over the words on a page. Deriving meaning requires making connections.

The more prior knowledge a reader brings to the classroom, the more he learns and remembers from what he reads. Since a lack of experience can become a barrier to learning new concepts or ideas, teachers need to find creative ways to help students develop and expand their knowledge base through direct exposure, discussion, analogies, and explanations for content area concepts. Content area teachers need to provide students a variety of opportunities to work with and experience these concepts in context and to explore relationships between them.

The first step toward this is to prepare students for reading by incorporating pre-reading strategies that activate and assess the learners' prior knowledge. This way, students can have a structure on which to attach new learning. Common pre-reading strategies used by content area teachers are:

- brainstorming

- asking questions

- providing analogies

- discussing the topic as a class

These pre-reading strategies benefit all students because those who have limited prior knowledge can learn from their more experienced peers. Students can even teach each other as they use these strategies.

Another benefit of using pre-reading strategies is the aid they can provide in helping teachers discover any misconceptions or inaccurate information students may have about a certain topic. As teachers use pre-reading strategies, students and teachers learn which strategies work well for them and the content area. Then, they can practice those strategies until they use them automatically when reading on their own.

Good readers know that they must think about what they are reading before, during, and after they read it. Many middle grades students are not aware of this need, and teachers must teach students how to monitor their own understanding at all three stages. By teaching students this approach, teachers help students consciously adapt and modify their reading according to what and why they are reading. Struggling readers have to be taught not only how to monitor their understanding, but also which strategies will help them most while they read.

2. The Classroom Learning Environment

Middle grades students must feel safe physically, intellectually, emotionally, and socially if they are going to learn in their classes. All students learn best when they feel accepted by their teachers and peers in an atmosphere where making mistakes and thinking in different ways is acceptable. Middle grades teachers especially need to create a sense of safety, acceptance, and order for their students.

Students will thrive in a classroom where they are given:

- **precise academic expectations and instructions**—explain what they will be doing with the information they read in the text (i.e., for a test, to write a paper, to give an oral presentation, or to present a project, and so on); explain necessary background knowledge prior to the reading if they do not have it

- **a purpose for the assignments**—explain why they are reading (i.e., to learn facts, to make a comparison, to look for the theme, for enjoyment, etc.). This determines which reading strategies to use, the pace of reading, the type of mental questions to ask and answer while reading, and how to monitor for understanding

- **the relevance of assignments**—explain what they will gain from learning the content (thereby increasing their motivation and interest); provide the opportunity for students to read text for real reasons

- **consistency and routine**—show students how to chunk work into manageable pieces and how to figure out what new words mean; teach them to follow a step-by-step process for analyzing and processing what they are reading

- **confidence in their ability to complete tasks successfully**—students learn best what is personally meaningful to them in a positive emotional climate

- **clearly articulated classroom rules**—content area classrooms need to become supportive environments for comprehension development

- **a chance to learn and interact together**—new learning occurs best when students have the opportunity to interact and share with each other. When students verbalize their ideas, it allows them to deepen their understanding and it also allows the other students an opportunity to compare their thinking and hear how others think with the teacher and with one another

3. Text Features

Reading comprehension strategies must be taught so students will have a solid foundation of skills to use as the text and vocabulary become more and more difficult. Students need to write about what they read and be motivated to use what they have learned.

Text features differ from subject to subject, so the reading skills and strategies students use will also change from subject to subject. Sentence structure and vocabulary are different. Science and social studies texts are often above the reading level of many students. While math books may have grade-specific math concepts, the reading level can be above that of the students as well. Again, when planning lessons, teachers need to look at their content as if they are the students rather than the experts. Which reading skills will the students need to understand what they are reading? Figuring out what skills they will need can be done by analyzing the text features of the books themselves.

Authors often organize their text by patterns. Common patterns found in textbooks are:

- comparison/contrast
- descriptive pattern
- episode pattern
- time sequence
- process/cause-effect
- general/specific patterns

Knowing which pattern is being used helps the reader to locate information, separate important and unimportant information, sequence events in a logical order, and link new information to what is already known. Content area teachers need to teach students the difference in narrative and informational text, typical patterns used in their textbooks, how to recognize the different organizational patterns, and the kinds of questions that each pattern is intended to help answer.

One of the most important aspects of text features is vocabulary. All content area teachers need to focus on vocabulary instruction. Each content has its own unique vocabulary, terminology, and language, particularly the labels used to identify important content area concepts. If students understand the content-specific vocabulary before they read, comprehension improves. Very often, content vocabulary consists of major concepts that set up a lesson or unit. Students must have a clear understanding of what these concepts mean. Also, content area vocabulary terms often need focused attention because they are rarely part of the content that students already know. Sometimes, content area terms are semantically related: if one science or math term is understood, others can be connected and understood.

Many teachers have students look up words in glossaries or dictionaries, but actually this is the *least* effective way to help students transfer the new words into their everyday language. Looking up a word does not aid understanding or long-term recall because it separates the learning of vocabulary from the subject matter. Just defining words is not enough to understand concepts. Students need strategies that can help them learn what new concepts mean and see the connections between these concepts.

Four levels of word recognition for students were identified by Dale & O'Rourke (1986) and Nagy (1988):

1. **Unknown word**—students cannot read or recognize the word.

2. **Initial recognition**—students recognize the word and may be able to pronounce it, but they do not know its meaning.

3. **Partial word knowledge**—students know the word in context and can use it in their writing.

4. **Full word knowledge**—students understand the meaning of the word and how it changes in different contexts.

Students develop knowledge about a new word gradually as they get repeated exposure to it. They move from not knowing the word at all to recognizing that they have seen the word before. Once the word is somewhat familiar, they develop partial knowledge where they have a general sense of the word means or they know at least one meaning. When students have full word knowledge, they know multiple meanings and can use the word in a variety of ways.

Teachers can help students learn new content-specific vocabulary directly through explicit instruction. They can teach vocabulary at the beginning of a unit of study, during the lesson, or after the text has been read. Regardless of the timing of the vocabulary instruction, students learn content area terms best through purposeful interaction with these concepts through field trips, guest speakers, or visuals like video, movies, or Internet research (Brozo and Simpson, 2003). After vocabulary terms are selected, teachers need to choose strategies that will help students learn the concepts and their relationships to each other.

Nagy, Anderson, and Herman (1987) identified six types of context clues that teachers can teach their students to use:

1. definition
2. example/illustration
3. contrast
4. logic
5. root words and affixes
6. grammar

No matter which vocabulary strategies content area teachers select to use, vocabulary must always be taught before, during, and after reading. Teachers need to make word study active. Students not only need to expand their knowledge of words, but they also need to understand words well enough to be able to use them appropriately during their everyday lives.

Teachers also need to limit the number of words taught at one time (quality not quantity) and concentrate on key concepts. The concepts need to be taught in semantically-related clusters so students can see related concepts. Teachers need to model how to determine a word's meaning in text material by thinking aloud and sharing the thinking process they use to understand the word with their students. Teach students not only how to use glossaries and dictionaries appropriately but also how to use those sources to figure out what new words mean.

Let's Play the Blame Game

In 1989, Irvin and Connors reported that, "Although it is unreasonable to expect that any student could acquire enough reading competence by the 5th grade to carry him or her through middle school, high school, and adult life, almost half of the middle schools offer no systematic reading instruction or make it available only for remedial readers or as an elective." This statement was made almost fifteen years ago, but, unfortunately, it seems that it still holds true today. In far too many middle schools, there are teachers who continue to believe that teaching reading is "not their job."

We have all heard colleagues say things like, "But I can't do everything! How can I be expected to teach these kids the curriculum *and* get them ready for state tests if I have to teach them to read at the same time? They should already know how to read when I get them! If their parents and the elementary schools had done what they were supposed to do, I wouldn't have these problems." For those of you who have heard these things said, let's talk about the blame game.

I am sure that when students arrive in kindergarten and first grade and are not "reading ready," there are some elementary teachers who blame the parents. Many of the parents who complain about teachers "not doing what they're supposed to be doing" may not have the knowledge or skills themselves to be able to help their children get ready to read. From the time these children are in kindergarten through 5th grade, teachers work hard to overcome the deficiencies (most out of teacher control) with which many of their students started school. And sometimes, no matter how hard elementary teachers work, some students still pass through to middle grades without being able to read at the appropriate grade level.

When these kids get to the middle grades, some middle grades teachers blame the elementary schools. The middle grades teachers work hard to overcome the deficiencies (again, most out of teacher control) with which many students graduated from elementary school. No matter how hard *they* try, some students still pass to high school as poor or struggling readers. Then, of course, when they get to high school, the high school teachers blame the middle grades teachers. Then, the high school teachers do *their* best to overcome the deficiencies with which the students arrive at high school. And, again, no matter what *they* try, some students still go on to college and have to take pre-college English, writing, and math classes before they can take college classes. It is a never-ending cycle of blame that can be stopped if all content area teachers realize that—regardless of what happened before—struggling or non-readers are *their* responsibility.

Good athletes (like Michael Jordan, Tiger Woods, and Wayne Gretzky) begin by learning the basics in their sports (like dribbling, putting, and passing the puck). These athletes practiced the basic moves until they became automatic habits. Once the basics were developed into second-nature, they were able to expand their skills and become superstars on the basketball court, golf course, or hockey rink.

In this same manner, middle grades teachers should think of their students as athletes at the beginning of their careers *in reading*. In teaching reading, teachers must take students through the same process that athletes experience. By teaching students to practice basic reading strategies in the content until they become automatic, students will gain the skills they need to become superstars in any subject or when they take standardized tests.

Harry Wong says, "The number one problem in the classroom is not discipline, it is the lack of procedures and routines." A similar thing may be said about reading: The number one problem with students is not their inability to read, it is their lack of basic reading strategies. The primary goal of all teachers is to make sure that their students will be taught reading strategies and then be able to use the appropriate reading strategies in each content area.

CHAPTER **2**

Creating an Action Plan

After examining the research and looking at what content area reading consists of, what do middle grades teachers do next? That's easy. With this newly developed knowledge, teachers can design an action plan for their classrooms that addresses four critical elements that are necessary in helping students with reading comprehension:

1. **A goal**—what do good readers do when they read in different content areas?

2. **An environment**—how can content area teachers create a supportive context for comprehension development in their classes?

3. **A model**—an overall view of how comprehension strategies are taught and learned. How can teachers design and implement activities that support the understanding of texts that students read in their classes?

4. **A curriculum**—which comprehension strategies will be taught, when, and how? How do teachers provide explicit instruction in the use of comprehension strategies for their students?

The rest of the book will help you develop your specific plan. Remember, you're not reading this whole book just to sit back and do nothing when you finish!

"One must learn by doing the thing. For though you think you know it, you have no certainty until you try."

— Sophocles (BC 495–406, Greek Tragic Poet)

CHAPTER **3**

CHARACTERISTICS OF
A GOOD READER

"One who fears failure limits his worth. Failure is the opportunity to begin again more intelligently."

— Henry Ford

What Makes a Good Reader?

Stop and consider what good readers do as they read, because the insights gained there can be used to teach reading strategies to students. Remember, understanding these texts comes easily to teachers because they love their subject areas, have college degrees, and may have taught the same grade and subject for years. It is easy to forget that when students read subject area content for the first time, comprehending what they read can be a consuming and complex activity. For good readers, reading for comprehension is a satisfying and productive process, but for struggling or non-readers, it is a painful experience not worth their time or energy.

 **DID YOU KNOW?** Without meaning there is no learning. It goes in one ear and out the other.

Good readers are engaged actively in what they are reading, and their minds have a movie playing as they read. They hear the characters' voices, see the setting, and participate in the events. This is why so many readers are disappointed when they see a movie or documentary of a book or something they studied or read: the scenery or actors do not look or sound like the people they had pictured in their minds when they read.

In fact, good readers in social studies and science can watch documentaries or scientific shows on Discovery, Biography, History, or even the Weather channels and question or discuss what they are seeing. Students must learn to read in different ways depending on the text, but good readers do some things consistently regardless of the text they are reading.

In general, good readers:

- **Make connections**—Good readers think about what they read and relate it to their own lives and experiences by connecting it to prior knowledge. Readers pay more attention to what they are reading when they can relate personally to the text. They comprehend better when they think about the connections they make between the text, their lives, and the larger world. They look for similarities between the descriptions in the text and what they have experienced personally, heard about the world, or read in another text.

- **Ask questions**—Questioning is the strategy that keeps good readers engaged. When readers ask questions, they clarify understanding and make meaning out of what they are reading. Good readers ask themselves lots of questions about what they are reading. Why is this event happening? What does this mean? Who says this is a good thing to do? Asking questions is at the heart of thoughtful reading.

- **Visualize**—Good readers create visual images in their minds based on the words they read in the text. The pictures they create enhance their understanding and help their brains remember what they are reading. They "see" the setting, characters, and events as they occur.

- **Draw inferences and predict**—Inferring requires good readers to take what they already know, gather clues from the text, and think ahead to make a judgment, discern a theme, or predict what is to come. Good readers wonder what is going to happen next, and they think about how things will turn out. They think ahead when they read and make guesses about what is happening so they can stay interested in what they are reading. They read on to see if their predictions were correct. In fiction, predictions are usually about future events or a character's thoughts, feelings, words, and actions. In non-fiction, predictions are usually about future events, people, places, and ideas.

- **Determine important ideas**—Good readers grasp essential ideas and important information when reading. Good readers are thoughtful readers and they are able to differentiate between less important ideas and key ideas that are central to the meaning of the text.

- **Synthesize information**—Good readers fit things together as they read and come to conclusions. They combine new information with existing knowledge to form an original idea or interpretation of what they are reading. Good readers think about what they are reading and form opinions. They review, sort, and sift through important information in order to gain new insights that might change the way they think. Good readers develop opinions about what they are reading.

- **Monitor comprehension and clarify**—Good readers know when they understand what they read and when they do not. They pull things together as they read to make sure that what they are reading makes sense. If it doesn't make sense, they have strategies to "fix-up" problems in their understanding as the problems arise. They try to answer any questions they have by using prior knowledge, context clues, re-reading, or other resources.

Because reading is an active process in which the reader must interact with the text, the following is a brief overview of what good readers do before, during, and after they read.

What Good Readers Do Before They Read

Even before reading a selection, good readers start asking themselves questions and thinking about what they are going to read. They set a purpose for their reading, preview what they are going to read, and plan how they are going to read. Good readers ask themselves these kinds of questions:

- What do I need to know before I read this material?

- What do I already know about the topic?

- How is the the text is organized to help me?

- What is the reason I am reading this material?

- What is the author's reason for writing this material?

- Am I reading for my own pleasure? If so, I can read at whatever pace I choose.

- Am I reading for school? If so, I have to ask some different kinds of questions as I read.

- Does the title tell me what the reading is about?

- Are there pictures, graphs, maps, titles, headings, bold face, or italics that can help me?

- Can I create a graphic organizer that will help me organize what I am going to read in a way that I can understand?

What Good Readers Do As They Read

Just like they do before reading, good readers have conversations and movies in their minds while they read. They read with a purpose and look for information that relates to that purpose. They try to connect the new information to other things they have read, heard, or experienced. They make inferences throughout their reading based on the background knowledge that they, personally, have. They visualize in their minds what is happening in the text as they read. Many good readers create sketches, concept maps, diagrams, charts, outlines, or notes as they are in the process of reading—visual ways to create and retain images in their minds. The visuals also help them identify the important elements.

As they read, good readers build meaning and frequently make predictions about what is to come. They read selectively, continually making decisions about their reading (what not to read, what to re-read and so on). Good readers construct, revise, and question the meanings they make as they read. They question what they do not understand or what is confusing to them, and they identify ways to figure out what has confused them. They draw upon, compare, and integrate prior knowledge with current material in the text. They think about the author's text, style, beliefs, and intentions. They monitor their understanding of the text, making adjustments in their reading as necessary.

Good readers try to determine the meaning of unfamiliar words and concepts in the text and they deal with inconsistencies or gaps *as they read*. They use context, syntax (the way a word functions in a sentence), and structural analysis of words to increase their vocabulary and to figure out new words. They evaluate the text's quality and value, and they react to the text both intellectually and emotionally. They try to identify, remember, and summarize major ideas for comprehension.

Good readers read different kinds of texts differently, so it is important for content area teachers to model and teach strategies on "how" to read in their particular subjects—use specific strategies for specific subjects. For example, when reading narrative text (as in an English class), good readers pay attention to the plot, setting, and characters. When reading expository text like in social studies, math, or science classes, good readers frequently construct and revise summaries of what they have read.

For good readers, text processing occurs not only during reading, but also during breaks in reading and then again after the reading is finished. While they read, good readers stop and ask themselves these kinds of questions:

- How does this connect to what I know?

- How does what I am reading compare to what I thought I knew?

- Does what I am reading make sense? If it does not, what is it that I don't understand?

- Do I need to code the text and note what is important, what I don't understand, what I need to re-read?

- Do I need to mark important words or ideas by highlighting, underlining, sticky notes, or transparent tape?

- Do I need to go back and re-read all or part of the material?

- Do the pictures, charts, graphs, or other visual aids help me understand what I am reading or give me more information that I need to know?

- Do I agree with the way the problem was solved? Am I surprised about the information? Is the information believable? Have I seen or heard something like this before?

- Are there clues for me so I can predict what the story is about and the problems that the characters will face? What descriptions do I need to remember?

- What is the plot or theme?

- What mental pictures do I see?

- What connections can I make from this passage to others that we have read in class?

- Who or what is the story about?

- When and where does the story take place?

- How and why do the events happen?

- Is there a specific problem that is solved?

- Do I see words that I don't know?

What Good Readers Do After They Read

After the reading is complete, good readers stop and reflect on what they have read. They identify things they have learned or are confused about, and they react to what they have read on an intellectual and emotional level. The goal of the good reader is to expand their base of prior knowledge and make connections to create new understanding. Good readers want to enlarge their vocabulary and thinking abilities, and be able to use the new learning in their thinking, writing, and talking.

After reading, good readers try to summarize main ideas and try to state them in their own words. They skim the text and often re-read the material to be able to meet the purpose of the reading and create a summary, an outline, a concept map, etc. After they read, good readers stop and ask themselves these kinds of questions:

- Did I find the answers to the questions I needed to answer?

- Did I learn what I wanted to learn?

- Were there other questions that I found?

- Were there questions or problems I didn't find?

- What do I know now that I did not know before?

- What is the most surprising or interesting thing I read?

- What new terms, concepts, or vocabulary did I learn?

- What do I remember?

- How do I feel about what I have read?

- Does my graphic organizer (if any) make sense?

- Can I restate the main points in my own words?

- How can I apply what I just read to my schoolwork and my life?

- Is there a lesson or moral in the story?

Surprising Things Good Readers Do

After reading this brief overview of what good readers do before, during, and after the reading process, here are some additional surprising things to consider about good readers. Like so many things in life, there are always myths or misconceptions that people have before they learn about something.

Myth One: Good Readers Skip Letters and Words

Contrary to what most people think, good readers do, indeed, look at all of the words and almost all of the letters in words when they read. The brain expects certain letters to occur in sequence with other letters, so it seeks familiar letter patterns in words. It is easy to assume that poor readers read slowly and choppily because they are looking at each word and letter, while good readers can read quickly because they skip words. This is not true.

Myth Two: Hearing Inner Voices is Bad

Good readers have an inner voice in their heads that they hear when they read. They hear words in their minds and this helps them create meaning as they read—different characters can even have different voices. It is easy to recognize students and adults who have not developed "inner voices" yet, because they move their lips or mumble as they read. Noticing this lack of inner voice is an important skill for middle grades teachers.

For example, have you ever instructed the class to read something silently, and some of them proceed to read out loud, in normal voices? When they would do that in my class, I would always say, "Class, remember you are to read this paragraph *silently*." The students who had been reading out loud would look up at me like I was crazy for reminding them. I thought they were simply being obstinate, but now I realize that these students had simply not developed their inner voices and had to read out loud so they could hear themselves and think about what they were reading.

There are ways to help students develop inner voices. Here are two that teachers can try:

1. **Change the way questions are asked.**

   Teach students to know that when a question is asked, no one is to blurt out an answer immediately. Instead, students should quickly turn to a neighbor and ask the same question of each other. When the pair is finished, they turn their attention back to the teacher, who then calls on one student to answer the question for the entire class. This process takes only a few minutes and accomplishes several things. First, the kids with no inner voices (who always blurt out answers) get to blurt at another student. (This way, they still get to hear themselves think.) Second, all the kids get to share their answers before sharing them with the class and very often a kid who is clueless gets to hear an answer that is at least on the topic from another student. Most importantly, this format eliminates competition for the teacher's attention between the blurters and the hand-wavers. All students get to contribute answers whether they are correct or not. Do not worry that students occasionally hear incorrect information using this technique. Remember, this is a management technique for kids who do not have an inner voice and who blurt out their thoughts all the time, not a Think, Pair, Share activity!

2. **Get them on the phone!**

Buy PVC elbows and make "phones" for students. When reading silently in class, ask students read to themselves using the phones. This keeps class noise to a minimum, and students still get to hear themselves read. Take it a step further and make the mouth and ear pieces turn outward so that two kids can read together—one reads while the other one listens and then they can switch. This works great and the kids love it.

Myth Three: Good Readers Always Use Context

Most good readers recognize most words quickly and automatically without using context. Context is used only after the brain has processed the word letter-by-letter. This is surprising because usually when students do not know a word, teachers automatically tell them to "sound it out" and then figure out what it means by using the context. It stands to reason that if the brain uses context only *after* it has processed each letter, then poor readers (who cannot read letter-by-letter) have almost no chance of figuring out new words by using context. In other words, good readers can self-correct their misreading because they are able to use context; poor readers cannot. Good self-correctors effectively use semantics (word meaning), syntax (how the word is used in the sentence), and their knowledge of letter-sound relationships. Therefore, telling a poor reader to "use context" to figure out a word is not likely to work.

Myth Four: All Readers Can Use Spelling to Learn New Words

The brain recognizes familiar spelling patterns, or words with similar patterns, that the reader has in memory. Good readers use spelling patterns and words they already know to help them understand new words. However, poor readers probably do not have enough words in their reading vocabulary memory even to recognize spelling patterns.

Good readers figure out big words by "chunking" them into manageable parts. They look for familiar parts of old words inside the new words. As Patricia Cunningham says, "In order to use known words to figure out big words, you must know some big words. Not only must you be able to read some big words, but you must also be able to spell those big words. The requirement that you be able to spell some big words along with the tendency of readers to guess or skip any word of more than seven letters may partially explain why so many older children experience problems reading their content-area texts." Poor readers just do not have the vocabulary reservoir to figure out big words.

READING
STRATEGIES

" . . . *effective teachers are able to craft a special mix of instructional ingredients for every child they work with . . . there is a common menu of materials, strategies, and environments from which effective teachers make choices . . . as a society, our most important challenge is to make sure that our teachers have access to those tools and the knowledge required to use them well.*"

— "Preventing Reading Difficulties in Young Children"
National Research Council, pg. 3

CHAPTER **4**

Strategies for Teaching Comprehension

Research has yielded several strategies shown to be effective when helping students develop comprehension skills. This chapter reviews some of the most common strategies. The first two strategies are some of the best instructional strategies that middle grades educators can use. All strategies are easy to incorporate in classrooms, start working immediately to help students read better in class, and are good choices when one is a new "content area teacher teaching reading."

Probably more than any others, middle grade students require active learning. They need to do more than worksheets. Further, all students have different personalities and learning styles, so classroom activities must include novelty and movement. Teachers need to create ways that students can associate the vocabulary of a subject with something meaningful. This way, students can do more than just memorize words, formulas, or concepts–and will be more likely to remember them.

After the new words are associated with meaning, there must be *practice* with those words (other than just looking at them in sentences and saying them). It is necessary to provide visual, auditory, and kinesthetic ways for students to learn and remember content-specific words.

Reading Strategy Number One: Learning Walls

This is a strategy that teachers can take advantage of with middle grades students, and it also is an easy thing teachers can do to assure administrators that they are teaching reading to students.

64   *How to Teach Reading When You're Not a Reading Teacher*

Learning walls will:

- provide a way for students to associate meaning with the words

- provide practice using a variety of learning modes

Some middle grades teachers, when first hearing about "learning walls" think "how elementary schoolish!" and worry that it sounds too much like being forced to have pretty bulletin boards. To many educators, having nice bulletin boards is nothing more than a way to make the classroom more inviting. Who has time to waste decorating a classroom when there are curriculum guides to cover, standards to be met, and state tests to address?

However, when examining the research about learning and the importance of brain-based instruction, the power of visualization as a part of long-term memory (and as a reading strategy) becomes clear. Any teacher who has posted a relevant chart or a graph on a classroom wall—and has then removed it for a test—has seen how students will look at the blank space as if the chart were still there. These students are "recreating" the information in their memories simply by glancing at the spot where the chart used to be.

At the beginning of the school year, it is easy to generate a list of essential words, concepts, formulas, or whatever their students must know in the content areas if they are to succeed in class during that year. This list of essentials is the perfect place to begin as the first content area reading strategy. After creating these charts, place them in a prominent place in the classroom where students will be exposed to them before, during, and after being introduced to the reading strategies.

Once a learning wall is set up, teachers will notice that their students use it as they are reading and writing. By using the brain-based ideas of color, location, and pattern, the recognition of elements becomes automatic. In this way, students can concentrate on content comprehension instead of being bogged down by the basics.

Selecting a Location for Your Learning Wall

Learning walls are not simply fancy bulletin boards, they are an important part of the learning process. Teachers should take advantage of the physical attributes of their classrooms and use desks, doors, cabinets, windows, ceilings, blinds, light fixtures, bookcases—whatever is available.

Put the learning wall anywhere the kids can see it. Incrementally, add pictures and phrases to the learning walls so students can look for (and find) patterns. Some teachers use file folders as "portable learning walls" for students to keep at their desks.

Teachers can also start simple when creating learning walls. Using 4 x 6 index cards, write the words on them, and stick them on the wall. For larger images, charts, or lists, use laminated and colored paper. Try using the same color for words that share the same concept; change to another color when the theme, chapter, or area of study changes. After all, since research has shown that the brain thinks in color, location, pattern, and odd numbers, give students access to all of it!

Selecting Words, Formulas, and Concepts for Your Learning Wall

According to Cunningham (1999), these are critical elements for using a learning wall:

- Be selective and include only essential words, formulas, or concepts that students need for your topic or subject

- Add words gradually—five words a week

- Make words accessible by putting them where everyone can see them, use big black letters and/or different colors

- Practice the word list daily so the words are read and spelled easily and instantly

- Make sure word learning wall words are spelled correctly in all student work

Select words that students will see and use often in reading and writing in your content area. Make sure to tell students that all of the words on the learning wall are important because they will see them over and over again, and that the terms will help them in their reading and their writing. Give the students an example of one of the words that is important because others have the same suffix or root, and then add or explain three more words or terms that have the same pattern. As there are the same words with different prefixes or suffixes, show them how the root word changes meaning.

 Black ink on yellow paper stimulates learning.

Making the Learning Wall Interactive

The more times a teacher is able to refer to the words on the learning wall, the more powerful it becomes as a visualization tool for long-term memory. Try to include an activity or comment about the words on the learning wall every day and have the students use the information. The more they use the words, the more they will retain them.

Here are a couple of ideas that teachers have used to make their learning walls interactive.

Guess the Word: This activity takes little pre-planning and could be a warm-up activity at the beginning of class to get students settled and on task.

Choose a word, formula, concept, etc. from the learning wall. Have students write the numbers one through five on a blank sheet of paper. Give five clues. By the 5th clue, everyone should have guessed the word. The first clue is always the same: "It's one of the words on the learning wall." Each clue will narrow down until only one word will work. Decide what students need to remember about the word and make the clues focus on that understanding. For example:

- "It's one of the words on the learning wall from this chapter."
- "It has four syllables."
- "It's only used when . . ."
- "It's part of . . ."
- "It completes the sentence . . ."

Wordo: Many people already do something like this since it is a spin-off of Bingo. It is a good test review game.

Make Wordo game sheets with the number of empty squares depending on the number of words you have displayed. Give students objects (such as beans or pennies) to cover the words as they identify them. Don't forget the "free space" in the middle. If possible, laminate the sheets so they can be reused.

Have students select and write words from the learning wall on their sheets in any of the blank boxes. Call out the words one at a time and the students can cover the words they have written. The first one that covers a row, four corners, the whole card, etc. wins—but only if the student can provide a *definition* of each word as it is called back. This encourages them to choose words from the wall that they know. You can do all kinds of things with this game, so be creative.

Reading Strategy Number Two: Sorts

Sorting is a wonderful activity to develop spelling, vocabulary, and comprehension skills. It works because students actively become involved in how words, processes, formulas, and concepts actually work within the content. In classes where sorts are regular activities, students start enjoying new words and ideas and begin thinking about where they fit into what they are studying. Reading and writing are connected to almost every lesson in content areas, so students learn to use what they know about these words and make connections as they read and write. Teachers can use multi-level sorts on the same concepts as a part of differentiating their instruction based on student need. Sorts can be done with words from the learning wall or any group of terms, words, or information that students need to memorize, label, or categorize.

First, decide the purpose of the sort. Is it to introduce new words or concepts or to be used as a review before a test? Then write 10–15 words, formulas, etc. on index cards or strips of paper. Have students sort the cards into different piles, depending on the criteria given them. It could be by term-definition, how the terms are alike or different, alphabetically, numerically, sequentially, chronologically—whatever works best for your content. Use sandwich baggies to put them in and make enough sets for students to work in pairs or individually. For those students who always finish their work before anyone else, give them a sort big enough to keep them busy. At times, teachers should allow students to determine which type of sort will be most effective. Students make some of the best sorts! Once again, if this process works well, start laminating, using colors, etc.

Other Strategies

Before their students ever read anything, most teachers begin by giving the students background knowledge and preparing them for what they are going to read. Teachers often go to great lengths to make the material interesting enough to grab student attention and motivate them to read the selection. Unfortunately, though, this tactic often gets students to read just enough so they will pass a test on the information. Obviously this practice does not always encourage student comprehension and critical thinking about the content.

The following are some common strategies to improve student understanding that teachers can use at any grade level or for any subject. Tierney and Readence (2000) tell us that these strategies will increase student-text interaction and comprehension and are designed to help teachers:

- activate students' prior knowledge
- foster active and engaged reading
- guide students' reading of a text
- reinforce concepts gleaned from the text reading
- encourage careful/critical thinking when reading a text
- pursue inquiry on different topics

Since these goals are important in content area reading, all teachers will find the following strategies useful. Some of them are easier to implement than others, and some of them may be more familiar than others. Keep in mind that any of these strategies can be modified to specific content. Sample forms for many of the strategies presented here may be found in the Appendix on page 129 of this book, and are intended to be copied and distributed to students.

Think Alouds

This is a modeling procedure designed to illustrate to students how to make connections to text. The teacher reads aloud from a text, stopping after a short passage, then "thinks aloud" showing how his brain makes connections that lead to better comprehension of the text. The only difficult part of this strategy for some teachers is

CHAPTER 4

that teachers are not used to "thinking about how they think," so explaining it to students is not an easy task. Although most teachers plan think alouds, they seem spontaneous to students. Think alouds are an important part of "how" to teach any comprehension strategy to students because they are a way of helping students monitor and improve their own comprehension.

In a Think Aloud, teachers model "fix-up" strategies for students. In other words, readers run into all kinds of comprehension problems in a text, so when teachers make their thinking public, they show students what to do when something is hard to understand.

For example, a teacher can show students how to:

1. Keep reading and see if the author explains what you don't understand.

2. Re-read to see if you missed something.

3. Read back to the part you didn't understand, or, read forward and skip confusing words.

4. Reflect on what you have read and see if there is an alternative explanation that can be inferred based on prior knowledge.

5. Seek information beyond the text (from a partner or a second source) in order to understand.

Teachers need to encourage students to do think alouds themselves when they read to help them clarify and sum-marize their thinking. As students think aloud, the teacher can monitor their understanding as well as see how they are thinking. Think alouds can easily be nested within any instruction, and they tend to make a teacher's oral reading exercises more engaging and understandable for all students.

How to Teach Reading When You're Not a Reading Teacher

KWL, KWHL, KWWL Charts

The KWL strategy (Ogle, 1986) provides a framework to help readers access knowledge about a topic before they read, consider what they want to learn, and then record what they have learned once they finish reading. It helps students reinforce the comprehension skills of questioning, predicting, clarifying, and summarizing. It also helps students focus on how they will learn the content and the graphic organizer helps transfer information to long-term memory.

Many teachers incorporate this strategy, but it has become more of a worksheet or something that is quickly put on the board rather than a focused comprehension tool. When using a KWL, teach the strategy first and make sure students understand the significance of the steps and how they impact on comprehension.

- **K** stands for **Know**—What do I already know about this topic? Before reading, students fill in this column to activate prior knowledge. (If they do not know anything about this topic, this is not a good strategy to use for this reading.)

- **W** stands for **Will** or **Want**—What do I think I will learn about this topic? What will I want to know about this topic? This is a prediction by the students based on a quick preview of the text to be read. This is a good time to use titles, headings, bold and italicized words, pictures, charts, graphs, etc. as clues. This helps set the purpose for the reading and focuses on key ideas. This step also helps students generate questions about the knowledge, and then read to answer those questions.

- **L** stands for **Learned**—What have I learned about this topic? After reading, students fill in their new knowledge gained from the content. This is a time to clear up any misperceptions or incorrect information about the topic. This is the meta-cognition stage.

Many variations of KWL are used. Additional columns can also be added, such as:

- **H** stands for **How**—How do I find the information? This column can be used by students who need to use a process or formula to comprehend the content.

- **W** stands for **Where**—Where do I find the information? This column is good because it allows students to brainstorm different sources of information at their disposal.

K	W	W	L
What I Know (Before Reading)	What I Want to Know (Before Reading)	Where I can find the Information (During Reading)	What I Learned (After Reading)
Put what you know here	*Write two or three questions you have here*	*Tell <u>Where</u> you'll look to find your answers*	*Write answers to your questions and important information here*
OR			
K	W	H	L
		Tell <u>How</u> you'll find the answers	
OR			
K	W	G	L
		Tell where you'll <u>Go</u> to find your answers	

OR
Create your own Chart!

How to Teach Reading When You're Not a Reading Teacher

Anticipation Guides

This strategy, developed by Tierney, Readence, and Dishner, can be used before, during, and after reading. Before reading, the teacher develops a guide of three to five statements that addresses issues related to the major topics or themes of the text. Make sure the statements on the anticipation guide present important generalizations about the issues that are worth discussing but do not have clear-cut answers. Try to make the statements debatable and experience-based.

In a pre-reading discussion, students will agree or disagree with the statements. Anticipation guides activate students' prior knowledge, encourage them to make a personal connection to what they will be reading, and give them a chance to become an active participant with the text before they begin reading.

Then, as students read, they can take notes on the three to five topics from their reading. Encourage students to read critically and try to understand the issues with an open mind or from different points of view. After reading the text, students review their original responses and see if they feel the same or they have changed in their thinking. The post-reading discussion gives the teacher a quick assessment of how well the students comprehended the text.

Anticipation Guide: helps students get interested in topics or subjects before they read. Works best when students have limited knowledge of the topic.

Students agree or disagree with each statement. Put A or D without discussion.

___ 1.
___ 2.
___ 3.
___ 4.
___ 5.

Make 3 to 5 statements that are important generalizations about the topic that are worth discussing and do not have clear-cut answers (yes/no, or one word)

After reading, use the following questions to discuss students guide responses:
1. Did we find answers to our questions?
2. What questions do we still have?
3. What information did we learn that we did not "anticipate" before we read?
4. What have we learned by reading this selection?
5. What was the most interesting, surprising, or unusual information you learned?

PIC: <u>P</u>urpose of the Reading
<u>I</u>mportant Ideas
<u>C</u>onnection to Prior Knowledge

This strategy is used before reading to help students activate background knowledge by previewing the text. This helps students focus on the most important information and allows them to make predictions and generate questions before they read. The goal is for students to understand what they are reading for and remember it after the reading. Model this behavior through a "think aloud" as you go through the text.

- **P** stands for **Purpose:** What is my purpose for reading? What am I going to do with the information when I finish reading? Will I write a paper, take a test, do a graphic organizer, do a project? How does this reading fit with the material before or after it?

- **I** stands for **Important Ideas:** How can I determine what important ideas are in the reading? Have students look at the title, pictures, headings, bold or italicized print, charts, graphs, maps, and sidebar sections. Is there anything in the table of contents, index, or glossary that can help me get the big idea? Are there questions to guide me in the reading? What are the key words I need to know?

- **C** stands for **Connection:** What do I already know about this subject? How does it fit with what I have already learned? What questions do I want answered? What does this remind me of? Have students develop questions they would like answered from reading the text.

After students read, have them go back and see if their predictions were accurate, if their questions were answered, and if they understood the important ideas based on their preview of the text features.

P	I	C
Put your <u>purpose</u> for reading here	*Write 3 or 4 <u>important ideas</u>, words, or concepts here*	*Write how what you already knew about the subject <u>connected</u> with what you learned*

3–2–1 Strategy

This strategy is to help students summarize key ideas, rethink the ideas in order to focus on the ones that they find most interesting or difficult to understand, and then ask a question about what they still want to know. Students fill out the 3–2–1 strategy chart with the following information:

- **3** things I found out from the reading
- **2** things that were interesting or difficult for me to understand
- **1** question I still have

This format can be used in a variety of ways. (**3** could be differences, **2** could be similarities, and **1** a question I still have.) Depending on what is being taught, the format can be modified. This strategy is beneficial because it is brain-compatible (containing odd numbers and small chunks of information) and it is a simple way to get students to differentiate between important and unimportant details.

The 3-2-1 format also can be used in place of worksheet questions, and the teacher can use student responses to construct an outline, make a graphic organizer, identify sequence, or isolate cause and effect. Student responses can form the basis for class discussion of the reading. The students are motivated because the discussion is based on the ideas that *they* found and consider important. This strategy encourages them to make a personal connection to what they have read.

3 ↓	Write 3 things I learned OR were new to me.
2 ↓	Write 2 things that were interesting OR were difficult for me to understand OR two key words OR important people.
1	Write 1 question I still have.

RAFT

A post-reading strategy, RAFT (Vandervanter and Adler, 1982) stands for Role, Audience, Format, Topic. This strategy gives students a structured way to format their writing, and it also allows them to be more creative in their thinking. It helps bring together students' understanding of main ideas, organization, elaboration, and coherence.

- **R**ole of the Writer: Who are you as the writer? A famous person? A character from the reading? A concerned citizen? A reporter?

- **A**udience: To whom are you writing? Is your audience a friend? Your teacher? Readers of a newspaper?

- **F**ormat: What form will the writing take? Is it a letter? A speech? A classified ad? A poem? A help column? A persuasive essay?

- **T**opic: What is the subject or point of this piece? Is it to persuade, entertain, describe, inform?

R	A	F	T
Write the role you will take as the writer here.	*Write the audience you are writing for here.*	*Write the text format you will use here.*	*Write your topic here.*

CHAPTER **4**

Graphic Organizers

A graphic organizer is a visual representation that shows how key concepts are related. Graphic organizers help students visualize connections between ideas. They can be called any number of names like pictorial organizers, webs, maps, diagrams, etc., but graphic organizers are visual ways to represent information. They help students organize information so they can make connections with what they already know. Selecting the right graphic organizer requires both the students and the teacher to use the structure of the text to help them understand and remember information.

The advantages of using graphic organizers with students in the various content areas are:

- There is little to read.
- They provide a way to organize content for better recall and understanding.
- They help kids "see" more abstract content, and technical terms can be taught in clusters to show connections.
- They are easy to construct and to discuss.
- Students can create their own.

Any piece of text can be displayed in more than one way depending on the purpose for reading. Graphic organizers can be used for planning, note taking, organizing, drawing conclusions, or assessing.

If you are creating your own graphic organizer, you can group information in a variety of ways such as:

- By main idea, sub-topics, and details
- In sequence
- To show relationships between different parts

How to Teach Reading When You're Not a Reading Teacher

- By components like the elements in a story
- By similarities and differences
- By cause and effect
- By stages of a process

After presenting different types of graphic organizers to students, it will be useful to have students begin to evaluate the usefulness of each different type of organizer. By doing so, students will learn to choose for themselves which organizer best suits the structure of the text that they are reading. Eventually students will be able to create and use their own graphic organizers. Let students read, take notes, then work in groups to create a graphic organizer to share with the class.

Cause-Effect   or   **If — Then**

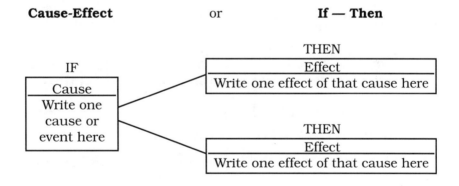

Problem-Solution

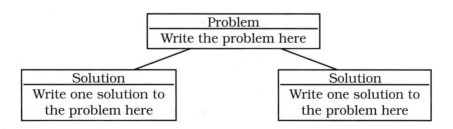

Column Notes

The column note format, based on the Cornell Note Taking System, has many variations depending on the purpose of the teacher and the material being read. Column notes best used when teaching advanced comprehension skills like cause and effect and comparison and contrast. Information is grouped according to type, then arranged in columns. Two-column notes are the easiest because students can fold the paper down the middle to create the columns. The number of columns can be increased depending on the type of information and the purpose of the notes.

For example, students can make column notes with:

- main ideas or headings on the left and details or explanations on the right

- cause on the left and effect on the right

- vocabulary on the left and definitions on the right

- questions on the left and answers on the right

- facts on the left and opinions on the right

- predictions on the left and outcomes on the right

COLUMN ONE	COLUMN TWO
Main Idea ⟶	Details
Cause ⟶	Effect
Vocabulary Word ⟶	Definition
Question ⟶	Answer
Fact ⟶	Opinion
Prediction ⟶	Outcome

Some teachers find it useful to expand to three columns and use a variety of headings. Example headings for three columns might include (but certainly are not limited to):

COLUMN ONE	COLUMN TWO	COLUMN THREE
Vocabulary ⟶	Definition ⟶	Sentence/example
Topic ⟶	Explanation ⟶	Supporting details
Questions ⟶	Notes from reading ⟶	Class discussion
Cause ⟶	Effect ⟶	Explanation
Key term/concept ⟶	In my own words ⟶	Picture
Process ⟶	Procedure ⟶	Results

The column note format is handy, and the organization of information is clear and much more visually useful for students.

QAR: Question-Answer Relationships

The QAR strategy (Raphael, 1982, 1986) provides students with a process to find and support an answer to a question. QAR encourages students to be strategic about their search for answers based on the relationship between asked questions and expected answers. Teach this strategy early in the year so students will learn how to generate different levels of questions as they are reading.

There are four types of Question-Answer Relationships. The first two questions are literal (in the text), and the second two questions are inferential (in the students' heads) and use their prior knowledge.

1. **Right There**—The answer is usually contained in a single sentence in the text and the words in the question are often the same words in the text. The answer is "right there." (I always point!) Right There questions begin with words like "who is," "what is," "how many," "name." The answer is usually one word or a short phrase, and there is only one correct answer. Sample questions are: "In what year did Columbus discover America?" or "Who was the sixteenth president?"

2. **Think and Search**—The answer is in the text, but you might have to look in several sentences to find it. You must "search" for the answer like a detective and "think" about how the information or ideas in the text relate to each other. Think and Search questions begin with words or statements like, "summarize," "retell," "compare," "explain," or "find three examples." A sample question is: "Compare the functions of roots to the functions of stems in a plant."

3. **Author and You**—The answer is not in the text but you must have read the text to answer the question. Readers still need information that the author has given combined with prior knowledge, in order to answer the question. A sample question is: "The topic of the passage was life in the eighteenth century. How does life today differ with life then?"

4. **On My Own**—The answer is not in the text, and in fact, reading the text is not even necessary to answer the question. It is based on personal belief and prior knowledge.

Visual Reading Guides

This strategy (Stein, 1978) is used to preview the selection to be read by noting the visuals provided in the text. Teachers help students identify important visual aids like maps, charts, graphs, pictures, cartoons, etc. that relate to the content or main ideas of the text. Visual reading guides help students understand the features of non-fiction text. Depending on the purpose of the reading, students learn to evaluate visuals based on their importance and quality. The teacher can do a think aloud to help students with questions such as:

1. How is the visual information related to the text?

2. Why did the author include the visual?

3. What does the visual show me?

4. How is the visual organized?

5. How can I use the information from the visual to help me understand what I'm going to read?

6. Why is the information from the visual important to the text?

After the teacher docs the think aloud, students should list two or three questions that arise from the visual aids and predict their importance to understanding what they will be reading. After the reading, students review the visual aids and decide if they did or did not provide important information.

Two examples of visual reading guides follow.

RIDER: A Visual Imagery Strategy

R Read the sentence

I Imagine a picture of it in your mind

D Describe how the new image differs from the old

E Evaluate to see that the image contains everything

R Repeat as you read the next sentence

AIDE: Strategy for Picture Interpretation

A Action—Look for the action in the picture

I Idea—Guess the main idea of the picture

D Details—Study each picture detail

E Explanation—Read the explanation with the picture

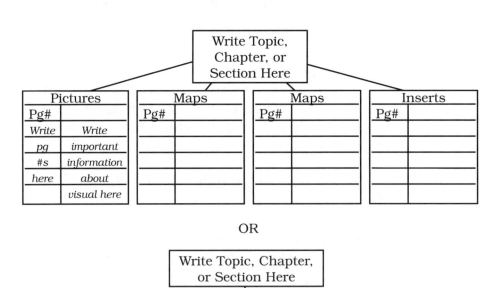

Pictures		Maps		Maps		Inserts	
Pg#		Pg#		Pg#		Pg#	
Write	*Write*						
pg	*important*						
#s	*information*						
here	*about*						
	visual here						

OR

Write type of visual here	Pg #	Write important info about visual here

Vocabulary/Concept Maps

Several mapping strategies were introduced during the 1970s and 1980s that help students acquire vocabulary and concept knowledge. These strategies were an alternative to the practice many teachers used of simply teaching and testing students on word definitions. Using vocabulary/concept maps builds on students' prior knowledge to help them see relationships with new words, terms, or concepts. In this way, students develop related—rather than isolated—word knowledge and develop skill in differentiating concepts as well as defining words. This strategy is particularly useful to teach vocabulary. Each mapping strategy can be used before, during, and after reading depending on the emphasis of the learning.

Semantic Mapping (Johnson and Pearson, 1978)

A semantic map, sometimes called a spider diagram or a semantic web, is a diagram with a key concept at the center and related concepts placed at the ends of radiating spokes. It is to make and use to show the connections between word meanings. Semantic maps help students organize what they know, so the words become more meaningful and memorable.

Semantic mapping can be used before or after reading, either to activate prior knowledge or to organize the new words that are learned. Stahl (1999) drew the following conclusions about the effectiveness of semantic mapping:

- Semantic mapping can improve word knowledge.
- Semantic mapping can improve comprehension of material containing the words included in the map.
- Group maps made by the students are more effective than providing ready-made maps.
- Poor readers benefit greatly from semantic maps.

A good way to make a semantic map:

1. Present a concept to students and have them brainstorm words that are related to the concept or topic being studied.

2. List their words, then add words students did not include.

3. Work with the students to develop definitions of the terms.

4. Place the target concept at the center of a diagram.

5. Get related key words and concepts from the students' list and place them radiating out from the central concept, grouping them into related categories. Make sure that a key concept anchors the end of each spoke and then draw a box or oval around it.

6. Introduce new words and related concepts attached to those known by students.

Semantic Feature Analysis (Johnson and Pearson, 1978)

1. Select a category of related terms.

2. List terms in a column.

3. List features (characteristics) to be explored in rows above the terms.

4. Indicate feature possession with + or –, or scale 1–3.

5. Explore new terms and/or features through discussion.

	Limestone	Basalt	Granite	Marble	Shale
Igneous	–	+	–	–	–
Metamorphic	–	–	+	+	–
Sedimentary	+	–	–	–	+

Word Concept or Word Definition Mapping (Schwartz and Raphael, 1985)

1. Identify a target word or concept.
2. Guide students to identify relevant (essential) characteristics and contrast these with irrelevant (non-essential) characteristics.
3. Generate examples to illustrate concept.
4. Attach concept to a larger category.
5. Consider related but different concepts within this category.

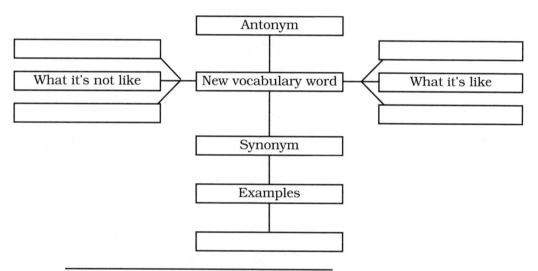

DISSECT Method for Vocabulary

D discover the context
I isolate the prefix
S separate the suffix
S say the stem
E examine the stem
C check with someone
T try the dictionary or thesaurus

Prefix   Stem   Suffix

How to Teach Reading When You're Not a Reading Teacher

CHAPTER **4**

Questioning the Author

This was a strategy designed by McKeown, Beck, & Worthy in 1993. Questioning the Author is used for students to think beyond the words on the page and to consider the author's purpose and effectiveness. Students are looking at the author's intent, clarity, organization, and anything else that they think writing effectively includes.

After reading the selection, students are to answer five questions:

1. What is the author trying to tell you?

2. Why is the author telling you that?

3. Does the author say it clearly?

4. How could the author have said things more clearly?

5. What would you say instead?

According to McKeown, et al, students should read text with a "reviser's eye." Sometimes when students have trouble understanding text, they assume it is because they are poor readers. McKeown, et al, see the idea of the "fallible author" and want students not to quit reading when the text becomes difficult, but instead to analyze what the author has done to make it so difficult for the reader.

Reciprocal Teaching

This strategy (Palincsar et al, 1984, 1986) is a compilation of four comprehension strategies: summarizing, questioning, clarifying, and predicting. Students need to have used all four strategies in their reading. One way to use this strategy is to have students read with a four-column chart with each comprehension strategy as a heading for one column. They can record what they do to understand the reading in each category.

Another approach is to put students in groups of four and identify each one in a role as summarizer, questioner, clarifier, and predictor. Students read a few paragraphs of the selection, take notes in their role, and underline or use notes to highlight key information. When they stop at a given point, the summarizer will give the major points; the questioner will ask questions about unclear parts, puzzling information, or new words; the clarifier will address the confusing parts and try to answer the questions; and the predictor will guess what will happen next or what will be learned as they read. If a reading is then divided into four sections, each student can have a chance to play all four roles.

ABC Brainstorming

This is a simple strategy that can be used before, during, or after reading. Students brainstorm a word or phrase associated with the topic to match with each letter of the alphabet. Before studying a major topic, use this strategy to check background knowledge. During the reading, it can be used as a way to summarize what students have learned to a certain point. After reading it can be used to create a summary or a review of the knowledge gained. It is most useful when the topic is broad enough so students can generate many possible terms.

1. Have students list the letters of the alphabet down a sheet of paper or give them a worksheet with the alphabet in boxes.

2. In no particular order, have students fill in words or phrases beside each letter.

3. Let students work individually at the beginning to give them plenty of time to think.

4. After they brainstorm alone, put them in pairs or small groups to compare answers and fill in any letters that were left blank.

5. Have students share their answers with the class.

6. At the end of the ABC Brainstorming, choose either to have students write a summary paragraph of what they think are the major points or create a graphic organizer of what they learned.

A	B	C	D
E	F	G	H
I	J	K	L
M	N	O	P
Q	R	S	T
U	V	W	X Y Z

Signal Words

Good readers adjust how they read text based on their purpose for reading. Signal words tell the reader the structure of the text so they will know how to think as they are reading. This will help them comprehend the text and be able to think more clearly about what is occurring in the text. Signal words help students predict, clarify, and question. They tell what is coming and what to watch for in the reading. Watching for signal words will focus the readers' attention and make them note the information to follow. The most common structures are:

• **the five W's and How**

Signal Words include: who, what, when, where, why, and how. These are the most commonly used signal words and learning them is a great way to start signal words because the are the questions that good reporters or detectives always ask to get to the most important details. Try drawing these on the fingers of a hand with "how" on the palm. Or say "Give Me 5" and the kids know to answer "The Five W's and How."

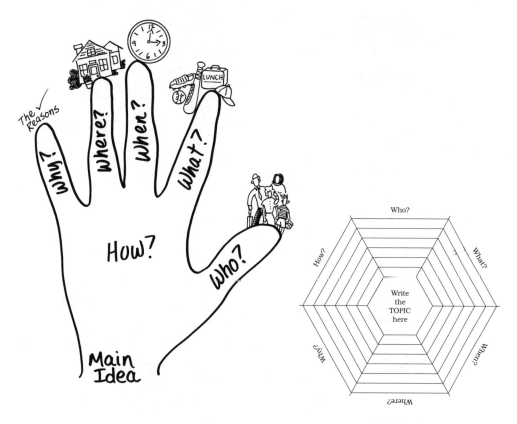

• cause and effect

Signal Words include: because, therefore, consequently, this led to, If . . . then, nevertheless, since, so, in order to, accordingly, because of, as a result of, may be due to, for this reason, not only . . . but, so that, and thus.

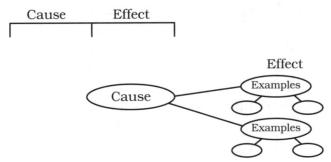

• compare and contrast

Signal Words include: different from; same as; similar to; as opposed to; instead of; although, however, compared with, as well as, either . . . or, but, on the other hand, unless, not only . . . but also, while, yet, but, and unlike.

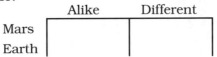

• description, problem, and solution

Signal Words include: the question is, a solution, problem, one answer is, and any of the signal words from cause and effect.

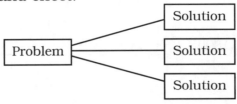

• description and enumeration

Signal Words include: for instance, to illustrate, for example, such as, in addition, another, most importantly, furthermore, first, second, to begin with, then, in fact, several, numerous, also, many, and few.

Items needed for camping:

1.

2.

3.

4.

5.

6.

7.

• sequence or chronological order

Signal Words include: not long after, next, then, initially, before, after, finally, proceeding, following, over the years, today, when, on (date), now, and gradually.

Beginning

Middle

End

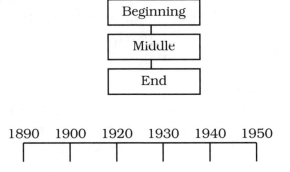

As students preview the text they look for signal words, generate a list then discuss what they think the structure will be. Students should be asking themselves:

- What kind of thinking will I need to do to understand the text?

- Which of the text structures is being used?

- How can I display the information after I read?

- What kind of graphic organizer can I create to visualize and connect the information?

After student discussion of the structure they have found (cause and effect, description, etc.), they can write one sentence about what they think the main idea may be. After reading, students can check their predictions of the main idea and then use a graphic organizer, write a summary, or in some way organize what they have read.

SCAMPER

SCAMPER is a mnemonic device developed by Eberle to help students expand and revitalize their thinking during brainstorming. It is a systematic way for students to generate new ideas or modify existing ones to encourage creative thinking. This strategy works especially well after students read.

S—Substitute—substitute something new in the passage to take the place of a character, event, location, time, etc.; have a thing or person act or serve in another's place

C—**Combine**—combine purposes, ideas, materials from the story; bring together or unite

A—**Adapt**—adjust to suit a condition, tune up or down, agree, reshape. (How would the story change if it were set in modern times?)

M—**Modify**—alter or change in form or quality; **Magnify**—enlarge or make greater in quality or form; **Minify**—make smaller, lighter, slower, less frequent

P—**Put** to other uses—use for a purpose other than originally intended

E—**Eliminate**—remove, omit, simplify, or get rid of a quality, part, or whole

R—**Reverse** or **Rearrange**—change order or sequence, adjust, create another layout or scheme

S	C	A	M	P	E	R
Substitute	Combine	Adapt	Modify	Put to other use	Eliminate	Reverse or Rearrange

CHAPTER **4**

SQ3R Reading Strategy

SQ3R is an acronym for the five steps that comprise a comprehensive reading strategy that has been around for years. It is not a difficult strategy to teach, and it helps students think about the material before, during, and after they read. The basic steps are:

S—Survey the reading material to get an idea about the nature of the content. Determine the structure, organization, or plan of the text. Details will be remembered because of their relationship to the total picture.

1. Think about the title. What information does it provide? Predict what will be included in the chapter. Change the title to a question that you need to answer as you read.

2. Read the introduction. The details will make more sense if you have an idea of the overall purpose of the reading.

3. Read the summary. Here is where you can get the relationship among the main ideas that were discussed in the introduction.

4. Read the main headings (bold face or italics). These are the main ideas and details that are in the reading.

5. Read the first and last paragraphs of the passage. Once again you will get the main idea of the text.

6. Check the source of the material, the date written, and the author.

Q—Question—Questions help the reader focus on ideas and details as they read. Questions become a criterion to use to determine if details are relevant or important.

1. Use the questions at the beginning or end of the text.

2. Formulate questions by changing main headings and subheads into questions. Example: Causes of the Civil War. What were the causes of the Civil War?

3. Formulate questions based on the first sentence of each paragraph.

R—Read the text with a purpose to answer the questions that you have made. Move quickly. Sort out ideas and evaluate them. If the content does not relate directly to the questions, move on. The key is to read selectively based on the questions you have developed.

R—Recite by making brief notes about the text or by using recitation (discussion) with a partner or in a small group. Think about the answers to your questions and answer the questions in your own words, not the author's. Write answers using only key words, lists, graphic organizers, etc. that will help you recall the whole idea.

R—Review what you have learned by re-reading your notes and by generating, answering, and discussing the questions. Try to recite the answers to your questions without using your notes.

DRTA

This strategy, Directed Reading Thinking Activity (DRTA), is used to stimulate students to become active participants in the reading process. It helps students set purposes for their reading and helps them comprehend what they are reading.

The steps are very similar to the KWL strategy:

1. **Pool Information**—Students combine their information and answer the question, "What do we already know about the topic?" This activates their prior knowledge.

2. **Develop Questions**—What do we want to find out about the topic?

3. **Search**—Read to find the answers to our questions.

4. **Analyze**—Which questions were answered? Which questions were not answered?

5. **Look Further**—Search for the answers to questions that were not answered.

Final Thoughts About the Strategies

Casey Stengel, a famous baseball coach, was talking about coaching a team when he said, "It's easy to get good players—getting them to work together is the hard part." To paraphrase and relate his sentiment to reading: "It's easy to find reading strategies, teaching them to students is the hard part." Teachers can find many comprehension strategies described in many places, and often teachers just take the strategies and use them with students *without teaching the students* the strategy. The problem is that too often students are not taught how to use these strategies when their teachers are not there making them do it. It needs to be made clear to students that these strategies are important for them to internalize so that they become a part of what they do when they read in all their subjects. For this reason, it is important to *teach the teacher* how to explicitly teach their students the strategies. The next chapter explains how to teach comprehension strategies and provides the script for a couple of samples.

DID YOU KNOW? The 80–15–5 Rule: Any one technique works great with 80% of kids, somewhat with 15% of pupils, and not at all with 5% of your students.

TEACHING
COMPREHENSION
STRATEGIES

"Learn from the mistakes of others—
you can't live long enough to make
them all yourself."

— Unknown

Questions To Ask Before Teaching Reading Comprehension

If middle grades teachers want to help their students with reading comprehension, they need to keep the following questions in mind before they teach a lesson:

1. Am I helping students activate or build on prior knowledge?

2. Is there active involvement by the students? Am I using student-centered (rather than teacher-directed) learning?

3. Do the students have time to work together during the learning process?

4. Are there opportunities for students to understand what (the content) they are learning, how (the process) they are learning it, and why (the reason) they are learning it?

5. Have I helped students analyze the text structure and how the information is organized?

6. Am I modeling strategies for my students and telling them my thought process and exactly what (and how) I am thinking?

7. Am I giving direct instruction of important vocabulary, concepts, formulas, etc. that allows students to be involved actively?

8. Am I intentionally teaching comprehension strategies to my students until their use becomes automatic?

9. Can I integrate the reading comprehension strategies before, during, and after reading?

Effectively teaching a reading comprehension strategy involves a number of steps. This chapter will provide a lesson plan format that will allow content area teachers to:

- Provide explicit instruction in comprehension strategies for their content using meta-cognitive instruction

- Explain, model, and guide practice until students apply strategies independently, flexibly, and in combination

- Provide instruction before, during, and after reading text

- Promote thinking and elaboration by asking questions, encouraging student questions and discussions, and using graphic organizers as scaffolds for thought

- Prepare for instruction by anticipating specific problems that students will encounter with content area text (prior knowledge/experiences, vocabulary, sentence structures, literary techniques, fluency)

- Use ongoing monitoring to inform instruction and measure progress

Meta-Cognitive Instruction

Meta-cognitive instruction of a reading comprehension strategy means that teachers provide a structuring mechanism to help students use the required strategy. This type of support helps students think about the strategy, plan the sequence of steps required in the strategy, and then monitors how they perform on each step. With consistent and regular practice in these techniques, students begin to develop their own meta-cognitive understandings, and they begin to generalize them across classes and content areas. Over time, even poor readers will be able to plan, organize, and complete reading strategies if trained to do so.

CHAPTER 5

Scaffolding

The kind of support teachers provide by using these teaching comprehension strategies is often called scaffolding. Scaffolding means that teachers give students verbal assistance, modeling, and graphic organizers— building on learning techniques to teach more effectively. In much of the content-specific reading that students do, there is an underlying structure that a graphic organizer will expose. This type of scaffolding is often called an advance organizer, and many of the comprehension strategies that are taught to students are types of advance organizers. A scaffolding organizer helps students to comprehend the basic organization of the material to be read prior to actually studying the material. It helps students connect new information to prior knowledge. Study guides, anticipation guides, chapter maps, and outlines are examples. These comprehension scaffolds can be based on words, on a reading skill, specific strategy, charts, pictures, labels, or a visual display of any kind.

With these techniques in mind, the following is a sample lesson structure that can be used when teaching a comprehension strategy. It is a combination of the Madeline Hunter six-point lesson plan and a variety of others. It is common practice for schools to have teachers turn in lesson plans, so substitute the appropriate words if they are different from the ones given here. Even when using the lesson plan format mandated by a particular school, try to incorporate the following steps until they become automatic when teaching reading strategies to students. Also, at the end of this chapter, two lessons are included that are scripted in this format, and sample handouts for the lessons can be found in the Appendix on page 129.

How to Teach Reading When You're Not a Reading Teacher

Lesson Structure for a Comprehension Strategy

Step One: Hook the Students

In this step, activate prior knowledge by connecting the strategy to something students already know or believe and get them emotionally involved in the lesson. Use humor, a personal story, or create relevance to their lives by telling them that knowing this strategy will help them get better grades, be better readers, historians, scientists, or mathematicians. The brain seeks novelty and students have to become engaged or they will not listen. This is a critical step in teaching a lesson because brain research shows that emotion drives attention, attention drives understanding and learning, and understanding and learning drive memory (Jensen, 1998).

If it is discovered in Step One that students do not have any prior knowledge about the subject (which is often true in middle school), give them a solid base of background information on which to build new material. Without making those connections, there may not be long-term memory.

Step Two: Whole Group Instruction

In this step, state the objective: to teach a specific reading strategy. Be very specific about what the strategy is, how the strategy works, and why it is important to know it in the particular subject area. This is the part of the lesson where students receive handouts, the teacher writes on the board or overhead, or whatever is normally done when teaching content. This is the teacher input part of the lesson. Remember to put some life into the presentation to keep the students' attention!

Step Three: Me (Think Aloud 1—Teacher Only)

Once the content of the lesson has been explained, the teacher models the skill or strategy and explains exactly what he is thinking (the process) using a Think Aloud. In this first Think Aloud, do not be tempted to include the students when modeling the strategy. Show them how a good reader in this subject "thinks." Of all the steps, this one is the hardest because teachers have always been taught to interact with students and keep them actively engaged. Some students will even try to "help" when their teacher first starts doing this Think Aloud process.

Another reason this first Think Aloud may be challenging is because it is difficult to explain the thinking process exactly. Many teachers have never thought it through themselves, so stop and figure out the steps before sharing it with students. Most of what the students will learn about the comprehension strategy they will learn from their teacher as a model. What they see their teacher do is what they will try to do themselves. Therefore, it is essential that the teacher be comfortable with the strategies and comfortable with "thinking aloud."

Step Four: We (Think Aloud 2—Teacher and Students Together)

This is the student interaction part in which students are engaged and think with the teacher using the Think Aloud strategy. The students have heard the teacher "think through" the process once, now they model the process again, this time with student involvement.

Step Five: Two (Guided Practice)

This step ensures that all the students participate. Use common sense to do what is best in a particular class during this step where the kids work collaboratively in groups of two or three. Remember, this step is *guided practice* so the teacher will observe or assist the kids as needed. This is no time to sit at the desk or do "administrivia." Teachers should use this step to assess the students' interactions to determine if they understand how the reading strategy works. If students do not get it, re-teach and do another Think Aloud before moving on to independent practice.

Step Six: You (Independent Practice)

If students do not seem to grasp the information at this point, go back and do *Step Three: Me*, *Step Four: WE*, and *Step Five: Two* again before continuing the lesson. Remember the old saying, "practice makes perfect"? That's certainly not the case here. What we know from the brain research is, "Practice makes permanent," so make sure students know and understand the reading strategy before they ever start the independent practice.

Step Seven: Closure

This is the time to review what students have learned about the strategy and discuss how they might use it when they are reading in other classes or are taking a test.

Teaching Reading Comprehension Strategies

Teach a comprehension strategy with content that all students can understand easily. The topic also should not be too interesting; otherwise students focus on *what* they are reading rather than on *how* they are reading. This is critical because the focus of the lesson *is* the strategy itself. Try using a story or a chapter that has already been read and even tested on to teach a strategy. This way the students think they already know the content, and they certainly will not find it overly fascinating reading. They will think it is easy to read and then they can focus on the strategy that is being taught instead of the materials.

When the lesson is finished, students should be able to describe the strategy they learned, how to do the strategy, and how it related to the text they read. They should not be talking about the content of what they just read.

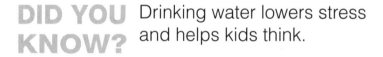

DID YOU KNOW? Drinking water lowers stress and helps kids think.

Here are some sample lessons illustrating two of the strategies discussed in Chapter 4 (QARs and Sorts). They can be customized to fit your content and teaching style.

Sample Lesson Plan 1:
QAR—Question-Answer Relationships

The objective of this lesson plan is for the student to be able to use the four types of Question-Answer Relationships to locate answers to comprehension questions. It is often necessary to teach QAR in two lessons. The first lesson plan focuses only on the two literal QARs, while the second lesson plan uses the two inferential QARs. Try teaching all four together and then separately to see which way works best for your classroom and students. Teachers are sometimes surprised by how difficult it is for students to differentiate between *Think and Search* and the *Author and Me* questions. That is why it may be necessary to use them separately.

Step One: Hook the Students

Sample Teacher Script:

"Have you ever had a teacher ask you to read something for a class, like a story or a chapter, and then you had to answer questions about what you read? Well of course you have; you're in school and that's what teachers do at school. But what I'd really like to know is: have any of you ever had trouble answering some of the questions and getting the right answers? Well, this kind of thing happens to everyone unless you know some tricks that good readers use when they answer questions. For example, sometimes the answer to a question is right there in one sentence of what we are reading, and it even has the same words that are in the question. At other times we have to come up with an answer for a question

by putting together ideas from several sentences that may not even be together in the same paragraph.

Today I'm going to share with you a reading tool or trick that good readers (historians, mathematicians, scientists) use when they have to answer questions about something they have read. It's called Q-A-R, which stands for Question-Answer Relationships."

Step Two: Whole Group Instruction

This is the part of the lesson where the teacher actually teaches the strategy. Give students a written and verbal description of each type of question-answer relationship. Give the students a handout with the four types of questions explained. Have each type of question written on card stock and laminated, so they can be put on the learning wall as each one is explained. Go over the handouts with the students and discuss the four kinds of questions. Consider using an overhead of the handout to teach from and refer to as each QAR is explained. Sample handouts are at the back of the book.

Step Three: Me (Think Aloud 1—Teacher Only)

Sample Teacher Script:

"Today we are going to read a chapter on the parts of plants. Now we read this chapter a few weeks ago, so I know that you all know what it says, and we already had the test. Most of you did well on that test, too. Well, almost all of you did well. At any rate, remember that

today we're not worried about what the chapter is about because our purpose is to learn how to read a chapter and then be able to identify what kinds of questions we are being asked to answer using Question-Answer relationships. After you learn the Q-A-R strategy, maybe on the next chapter, you will be able to answer every question on the test correctly, and everybody will make an A. I think that would be great! So, the first thing a good reader always does is read the questions at the end of the chapter before he ever starts reading. This way, we'll know exactly what it is that we are reading to learn.

After we read the questions, I'm going to read the first few paragraphs aloud to you, and I want you to follow along with me as I read. After I finish reading the first few paragraphs, I'm going to model for you what I would do, how my brain would be thinking, to answer the questions at the end of the chapter using the four kinds of Q-A-R questions."

Step Four: We (Think Aloud 2—Teacher and Students Together)

Sample Teacher Script:

"Now that I've shown you how I would use the four kinds of Q-A-Rs on these first two paragraphs, we're going to read the next two paragraphs together. I'll read aloud and you follow along with me. When we finish reading, we'll practice the questions together and see if you understand how to do Q-A-Rs."

After reading the passage, ask one question from each QAR category. Point out the differences between each question and the type of answer it requires. You may have to do this several times.

After students demonstrate that they understand the differences among the four QAR levels, go to the next part of the lesson.

Step Five: Two (Guided Practice)

Sample Teacher Script:

"You guys did a great job with those paragraphs, so now you're going to work with a partner and make up four questions, one for each kind of Q-A-R, from the next two paragraphs in the chapter. First you will read the paragraphs together just like we did as a class. Each one of you will read a paragraph out loud while your partner follows along. When you have both read your paragraphs, here's what I want you to do . . . "

1. *Read the assigned paragraphs with your partner. Remember that each person must read at least one paragraph out loud while the partner follows along.*

2. *When you finish reading, you will work together and make up four questions—one for each Q-A-R—and write them on your individual papers.*

3. *For each question you will:*

   • *Write which type of Q-A-R it represents.*

   • *Write where the answer to the question is found in the paragraphs (paragraph and line). You don't have to copy the sentence from the paragraphs.*

   • *Write why (the reasons) the questions represent one Q-A-R but not another.*

When everyone is finished, you and your partner will share your questions with another pair of students and see if they can identify your Q-A-Rs."

After students have done this step, discuss as a class what each group considers their best question for each level of QAR.

Step Six: You (Independent Practice)

If time permits in class, have students read more of the chapter alone and then write two questions, tell what kind of QAR each one is, tell why the question represents a certain QAR, and tell where the information is in the passage. If the students understand the strategy, assign this for homework.

Step Seven: Closure

Sample Teacher Script:

"You guys did great today. Let's quickly review the four kinds of question-answer relationships. Now that you know what it is, what do you think about Q-A-R? Is it something you think will help you in other classes? Explain why (the reasons) you think that. Will it help you when you take tests? Why do you think it will/won't?"

Sample Lesson Plan 2:
Sort Activity for Math Vocabulary

The objective of this lesson is for the student to be able to match math terms and definitions/formulas using a sort activity. This activity can be used before teaching the chapter as a pre-assessment of prior knowledge or as a reinforcement or review.

Step One: Hook the Students

Sample Teacher Script:

"Have you ever noticed how many words are in the math textbook? Not only do you have to know numbers and math formulas, but you also have to know math terms. Sometimes it is very difficult to keep all the formulas and terms straight. Remember when you were first learning your timetables in elementary school? I bet one of the things you did to memorize them was to use flash cards, or maybe you had to write them over and over. We've covered a lot of material in this chapter and some of it is confusing, so today we're going to use a strategy that many mathematicians use when they need to remember a lot of important math information. It is an activity that will help you remember the important terms and formulas for this chapter. We are going to do a math sort! It is a way of categorizing or grouping our terms and formulas so we can remember them."

See sample math sort at back of book.

Step Two: Whole Group Instruction

In this lesson, use terms and formulas with their definitions. Use one color of paper for the terms/formulas and another color for the definitions. Make enough sets for students to work in pairs with a few extra just in case. As usual, laminate the sheets before they are cut up. Make one set of example terms/formulas that are different from the ones the students will do to use when modeling for them how to do a sort in *Step Three: Me (Think Aloud 1—Teacher Only)*.

Sample Teacher Script:

"I bet you've sorted lots of things before. Anybody have to do their own laundry at home? Do you put all the clothes together when you wash them, or do you sort them into groups by colors? Well, a sorting activity is exactly the same idea. I have a baggie with terms, formulas, and definitions in it. The purpose of this kind of sort is to match the terms or formulas with their definitions. First, I'm going to show you how I would do a sort like this."

Step Three: Me (Think Aloud 1—Teacher Only)

Sample Teacher Script:

"I bet you're thinking 'Why does she need to show us how to do this? After all, how hard can it be to dump out some terms and definitions and match them up?' Well, that's exactly why I'm going to show you how a mathematician would do this sort. There is thinking involved!

O.K., I get my baggie and notice that there are two different colors of paper in it. Hmmm. I wonder if that's important or means anything. I guess I'll take a look and see. Oh, I see—the terms and formulas are one color and the definitions are another. That's good to know and that should help me. I think I'll start with the ones I know and then go to the hard ones. In fact, I think I'll make three stacks as I take out the terms or formulas. I'm going to put the ones I know for sure in one stack, the ones I think I know in another, and the ones I'm clueless about in a third stack. This way I can work quickly when I take out the definitions. I'll be able to match them up easily with the ones I know and then guess with the ones that are left over."

As you talk this through, use the samples from your baggie. Make sure to have a few extra to do with the students in the next think aloud.

Step Four: We (Think Aloud 2—Teacher and Students Together)

Sample Teacher Script:

"Now that I've shown you how I would do this activity, let's match a few together."

Step Five: Two (Guided Practice)

Sample Teacher Script:

"O.K. you are ready to work together. I've got a baggie for each pair, but don't open your baggie until everyone gets theirs. I want you all to start together and see which team finishes first. Ready, go."

Step Six: You (Independent Practice)

Sample Teacher Script:

"Now that you know how a sort works for remembering math terms and formulas, I want you to think of three words or formulas that I didn't include in my sort. Think of three words or formulas that you think are important and put them on these index cards. Write the term or formula on one index card and put the definition on another. When everyone finishes, you'll share them with your partner and see if he knows them."

Step Seven: Closure

Sample Teacher Script:

"Good job today. Do you think doing sorts will help you remember math terms and formulas from now on? Is this a good way to review for a test? We're going to make up some new sorts using the words each of you came up with today, and use sorts again when we have time."

CHAPTER **5**

Final Thoughts on Teaching
Reading Comprehension Strategies

Reading to learn content is an interactive process with three distinct phases: before-reading, during-reading, and after-reading. In order for students to engage actively in reading the content of their subjects, which often contains new information and subject-specific language, is difficult to understand, and not written in an exciting way, teachers must use the reading comprehension strategies that are most effective in their subject areas. When beginning to choose which comprehension strategies to use, the following guidelines may be helpful:

- Select strategies that are used by readers of the subject in real life

- Comprehension strategies should be taught over time during the year

- Teach one strategy at a time

- Strategies need to be explicitly taught in the context of reading the content

- Each new strategy needs to be modeled and explained

- Supported, structured practice of each strategy needs to be provided (scaffolding)

- Plenty of practice is provided for each strategy

- Students need to learn that reading is highly personal because it is a reflective and intentional process

- Comprehension strategies need to be taught and used throughout the school day in all content areas to show how they are effective with any subject

How to Teach Reading When You're Not a Reading Teacher

When using these guidelines to help select strategies to teach students, remember that for the before-reading phase, content teachers need to teach strategies that get students to think not only about what they are going to read, but more importantly, about *how* they will read it. Teachers must help their students learn how to prepare for learning in content areas through

- teaching pre-reading comprehension strategies

- ensuring comprehension during the reading by using meta-cognitive strategies and scaffolding

- extending and refining the new knowledge students acquire after reading

"If you can imagine a thing, conjure it up in space, then you can make it . . . The universe is real but you can't see it. You have to imagine it. Then you can be realistic about reproducing it."

— Alexander Calder, sculptor

CONCLUSION

"We can't keep teaching the same old ways, Cause if we keep on doing what we've always been doing, we'll keep on getting what we've always been getting."

— Unknown

CHAPTER **6**

The Learning Process and How to Teach It

As stated earlier, in order for middle grades students to become successful readers in their subject areas, every teacher must become not only a teacher of their own subject area but also a teacher of reading comprehension strategies. Since good readers use a variety of strategies when they read to make sense out of what they are reading, it is the teacher's responsibility to help students be aware of the strategies that work best well in their content. The strategies chosen to teach students need to be flexible and adaptable to meet the needs of any reading problem regardless of the content.

In his book, *Powerful Learning*, Ron Brandt summarized the learning process with the following statements:

1. People learn what is personally meaningful to them.

2. People learn when they accept challenging but achievable goals.

3. Learning is developmental.

4. Individuals learn differently.

5. People construct new knowledge by building on their current knowledge.

6. Much learning occurs through social interaction.

7. People need feedback to learn.

8. Successful learning involves the use of strategies—which themselves must be learned.

9. A positive emotional climate strengthens learning.

10. Learning is influenced by total environment.

These ten statements summarize not only the learning process, but also clarify what this book has to say about teaching reading.

It is helpful to remember the critical questions that must be addressed by content area teachers as they become teachers of reading strategies:

1. **What do good readers in my content area do as they read?**
   Finding out this information and modeling it is your goal.

2. **How can I create a supportive context for comprehension development in my classroom?**
   A supportive environment allows students to believe that they really can learn to read the text in a particular subject.

3. **How can I design and implement activities that will support reading comprehension? Which format or lesson plan will I use?**
   This is the model of what you plan to do, and it forces you to plan to intentionally and explicitly include reading strategies in your lessons.

4. **Which comprehension strategies will I teach? When will I teach them? How will I teach them? How will I provide explicit instruction in the use of reading comprehension strategies for my students?**
   This is the broadening of your content area curriculum. You know your subject area scope and sequence, so the hard part will be deciding how to use your content as a vehicle to also teach reading strategies.

There are many other strategies available that will work with middle grades students. For an extended listing of these resources, see the bibliography at the end of this book.

Creating a Personal Action Plan for Yourself

Now that you have read *How to Teach Reading When You're Not a Reading Teacher*, it is time for you to develop a personal action plan. Using prior knowledge and knowledge gained from reading this book, you are ready to begin a very rewarding phase in your teaching career. You will no longer only be an English, Math, Science, or Social Studies teacher. Instead, you will be able to say that you are an English, Math, Science, or Social Studies teacher who teaches reading!

There is an action plan form for use at the end of this chapter. Take the time to think it through and fill it out. When students can read in the content areas, they learn to love it like their teachers do! Most importantly, do not get discouraged if everything does not work exactly right the first time.

My Personal Action Plan

Success always begins with a plan. Once a personal action plan is developed and put into writing, follow-through is more likely. Answer the four questions below and then sign and date your commitment. During the year, try to teach your students at least one comprehension strategy each grading period.

My Goal: What do good readers in my subject do when they read?

_____
_____
_____

The Environment: How can I change my classroom setting or routine to help me teach my students to read better? How can I create a supportive environment?

_____
_____
_____

The Model: How can I design and implement activities that will help reading comprehension? What format or lesson plan will I use?

_____
_____
_____

The Curriculum: Which strategies will I teach? When will I teach them? How will I teach them?

_____
_____
_____

Signature_____ **Date**_____

APPENDIX

QAR — Question-Answer Relationships

## Literal (Text)	## Inferential (Knowledge)

Right There

The answer is "right there" in the text and you can point to the words! It is easy to find the answer because the question uses the same words that are in the answer. The answer is in <u>one</u> sentence in the passage.

Author and Me

You must use what the author tells you in the text, plus what you already know to get the answer. The answer is not written down in the text. You must put the information from the text with what you know to get the answer.

Think and Search

The answer will be pieced together by combining information from two or more sentences. It is in the text, but you must "think" and then "search" for the answer.

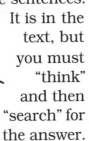

On My Own

The answer is not in the text. You must use your own prior experiences and background to get the answer. You must think about what you know to get the answer.

How to Teach Reading When You're Not a Reading Teacher

Math Sort

MONOMIAL	**Product of numbers and variables**
BINOMIAL	**Sum or difference of 2 monomials**
TRINOMIAL	**Sum or difference of 3 monomials**
PRIME NUMBER	**A number with exactly 2 factors ("1" and itself)**
RATIO	**Two numbers, division, comparison, colon**
SIMILAR	**Same shape, different size**

How to Teach Reading When You're Not a Reading Teacher

COMPLEMENTARY ANGLES	**Sum of measures is 90 degrees**
SUPPLEMENTARY ANGLES	**Sum of measures is 180 degrees**
PYTHAGOREAN THEOREM	**Variables, triangle, right angle, hypotenuse, squared numbers, named after someone**
TRANSLATION	**Slide—requires: direction and number of units**
ROTATION	**Turn—requires: points of rotation, direction, and angles of rotation**
REFLECTION	**Flip—requires: line of reflection**

MEAN	**Average**
MODE	**Data item that appears the most**
FACTOR	**Write a multiplication problem for which you have the answer**
MEDIAN	**Middle number of arranged data**
PROBABILITY	**# of favorable outcomes** / **# of possible outcomes**

BIBLIOGRAPHY

Allen, Janet. *It's Never Too Late: Leading Adolescents to Lifelong Literacy.* Portsmouth, NH: Heinemann, 1995.

Allen, Janet. *Words, Words, Words: Teaching Vocabulary in Grades 4–12.* Portland, ME: Stenhouse Publishers, 1999.

Barton, M.L. "Addressing the Literacy Crisis: Teaching Reading in the Content Areas," *NASSP Bulletin* 81:587 (1997), 22–30.

Beers, Kylene. *When Kids Can't Read: What Teachers Can Do.* Portsmouth, NH: Heinemann, 2003.

Blevins, Wiley. *Building Fluency: Lessons & Strategies for Reading Success.* Jefferson City, MO: Scholastic Professional Books, 2001.

Blevins, Wiley. *Teaching Phonics & Word Study in the Intermediate Grades.* Jefferson City, MO: Scholastic Professional Books, 2001.

Brandt, Ron. *Powerful Learning.* Alexandria, VA: Association for Supervision & Curriculum Development, 1998.

Buehl, Doug. *Classroom Strategies for Interactive Learning,* 2d Ed. Newark, DE: International Reading Association, 2001.

Burns, M. Susan, Peg Griffin, and Catherine Snow, eds. *Starting Out Right: A Guide to Promoting Children's Reading Success.* Washington DC: National Academy Press, 1999.

Cochran, Judith. *As Reading Programs Come and Go This Is What You Need to Know.* Nashville: Incentive Publications, 2002.

Covey, Stephen. *The Seven Habits of Highly Effective People.* New York: Simon & Schuster, 1989.

Cunningham, Patricia M. *Phonics They Use: Words for Reading and Writing.* New York: Longman, 2000.

Forte, Imogene. *Language Literacy Lessons: (Series)* Nashville: Incentive Publications, 2002.

Forte, Imogene. *Lecciones de Lenguaje: (Series)* Nashville: Incentive Publications, 2002.

Forte, Imogene and Marjorie Frank. *If You're Trying to Get Better Grades and Higher Test Scores in Reading and Language, You've Gotta Have This Book!* Nashville: Incentive Publications, 2002.

Forte, Imogene and Sandra Schurr. *Standards-Based Graphic Organizers, Rubrics, and Writing Prompts for Middle Grades Students in Language Arts, Math, Science, and Social Studies.* Nashville: Incentive Publications, 2003.

Frender, Gloria. *Learning to Learn: Strengthening Study Skills and Brain Power.* Nashville: Incentive Publications, 1990.

Gregory, Gayle and Carolyn Chapman. *Differentiated Instructional Strategies: One Size Doesn't Fit All.* Thousand Oaks, CA: Corwin Press, 2002.

Hollimon, L. *The Complete Guide to Classroom Centers.* Creative Teaching Press, Inc. Cypress, CA: Creative Teaching Press, 1996.

Jensen, Eric. *Teaching with the Brain in Mind.* Alexandria, VA: Association for Supervision and Curriculum Development, 1998.

Marzano, Robert, Debra Pickering, and Jane Pollock. *Classroom Instruction That Works.* Alexandria, VA: Association for Supervision and Curriculum Development, 2001.

Moore, David, John Readence, and Robert Rickelman. *Prereading Activities for Content Area Reading and Learning.* Newark, DE: International Reading Association, 2000.

Nagy, William. *Teaching Vocabulary to Improve Reading Comprehension.* Newark, DE: International Reading Association, 1988.

Pearson, P.D., and Johnson, D.D. *Teaching Reading Comprehension.* New York: Holt, Rinehart and Winston, 1978.

Robb, Laura. *Teaching Reading in Middle School.* New York: Scholastic Professional Books, 2000.

Schwartz, Robert M., and Taffy Raphael. "Concept of Definition: A Key to Improving Students' Vocabulary." *Reading Teacher,* 39 (2) (1985), 198–205.

Shalaway, Linda and Linda Beech. *Learning To Teach . . . Not Just for Beginners.* New York: Scholastic Professional Books, 1998.

Silver, Debbie. *Drumming to the Beat of a Different Marcher: Finding the Rhythm for Teaching a Differentiated Classroom.* Nashville: Incentive Publications, 200.

Snow, Catherine, M. Susan Burns, and Peg Griffin, eds. *Preventing Reading Difficulties in Young Children.* Washington DC: National Academy Press, 1999.

Sousa, David. *How the Brain Learns.* Thousand Oaks, CA: Corwin Press, 2001.

Stahl, Steven. *Vocabulary Development: From Research to Practice.* vol. 2. Cambridge, MA: Brookline Books, 1999.

Tierney, Robert and John Readence. *Reading Strategies and Practices: A Compendium.* 5th ed. Boston: Allyn and Bacon, 2000.

Tomlinson, Carol Anne. *The Differentiated Classroom: Responding to the Needs of All Learners.* Alexandria, VA: Association for Supervision and Curriculum Development, 1999.

Tovani, Cris. *I Read it, But I Don't Get It: Comprehension Strategies for Adolescent Readers.* Portland, ME: Stenhouse Publishers, 2000.

Vacca, Richard and Jo Anne Vacca. *Content Area Reading.* 4th ed. New York: Harper Collins, 1993.

Walberg, Herbert J. Walberg and Shiow-Ling Tsai, "Matthew Effects in Education," *American Educational Research Journal,* 1983, 20:359-373.

Wolfe, Patricia. *Brain Matters: Translating Research into Classroom Practice.* Alexandria, VA: Association for Supervision and Curriculum Development, 2001.